# Spring
*A Developer's Notebook*™

# Other Java™ resources from O'Reilly

| | | |
|---|---|---|
| **Related titles** | Java™ in a Nutshell | Jakarta Struts Cookbook™ |
| | Head First Java™ | Tomcat: The Definitive Guide |
| | Head First Design Patterns | Learning Java™ |
| | Hibernate: A Developer's Notebook™ | Java™ Extreme Programming Cookbook™ |
| | Programming Jakarta Struts | Hardcore Java™ |

**Java Books Resource Center**

*java.oreilly.com* is a complete catalog of O'Reilly's books on Java and related technologies, including sample chapters and code examples.

*OnJava.com* is a one-stop resource for enterprise Java developers, featuring news, code recipes, interviews, weblogs, and more.

**Conferences**

O'Reilly Media, Inc. brings diverse innovators together to nurture the ideas that spark revolutionary industries. We specialize in documenting the latest tools and systems, translating the innovator's knowledge into useful skills for those in the trenches. Visit *conferences.oreilly.com* for our upcoming events.

Safari Bookshelf (*safari.oreilly.com*) is the premier online reference library for programmers and IT professionals. Conduct searches across more than 1,000 books. Subscribers can zero in on answers to time-critical questions in a matter of seconds. Read the books on your Bookshelf from cover to cover or simply flip to the page you need. Try it today with a free trial.

# Spring

*A Developer's Notebook*™

**Bruce A. Tate and Justin Gehtland**

**O'REILLY**®

*Beijing · Cambridge · Farnham · Köln · Paris · Sebastopol · Taipei · Tokyo*

**Spring: A Developer's Notebook**™
by Bruce A. Tate and Justin Gehtland

Copyright © 2005 O'Reilly Media, Inc. All rights reserved.
Printed in the United States of America.

Published by O'Reilly Media, Inc., 1005 Gravenstein Highway North, Sebastopol, CA 95472.

O'Reilly books may be purchased for educational, business, or sales promotional use. Online editions are also available for most titles (*safari.oreilly.com*). For more information, contact our corporate/institutional sales department: (800) 998-9938 or *corporate@oreilly.com*.

| | |
|---|---|
| **Editor:** | Mike Loukides |
| **Production Editor:** | Colleen Gorman |
| **Cover Designer:** | Emma Colby |
| **Interior Designers:** | David Futato and Edie Freedman |

**Printing History:**

| | |
|---|---|
| April 2005: | First Edition. |

 This book uses RepKover™, a durable and flexible lay-flat binding.

ISBN: 0-596-00910-0
[M]

# Contents

# Foreword

Bruce Tate is a great communicator—as you'll know if you've been fortunate enough to hear him present. His communication skills also shine in his books, and this is another fine example. It's well written and to the point. It's also enjoyable to read, and that's important.

With *Spring: A Developer's Notebook*, Bruce Tate and Justin Gehtland offer a great way to get started with the Spring Framework. You'll find the consistent structure helpful, as it takes you step-by-step through important development activities. You'll find many code examples demonstrating exactly how to use Spring to address common requirements. Although Spring has a large and growing literature, with more books coming out every quarter, this one fills an important gap. If you're new to Spring and need to get started quickly, you need this book.

When I wrote *Expert One on One J2EE Design and Development* in 2002, I never imagined that the core code from that book would become one of the most important open source frameworks in the world, in the form of the Spring Framework. But it has. Major corporations now use Spring in many different industries and technological environments. Spring powers critical applications in some of the largest banks in Europe and North America. Spring powers logistics applications and enrollment and purchasing systems at major universities. Spring is used in some of the world's leading scientific research organizations. Spring empowers Grid computing, dealer relationships, and countless start-up businesses. It's easy to see why:

- Spring is much simpler than traditional J2EE alternatives. With Spring, you code your applications as plain old Java objects (POJOs), while still enjoying sophisticated transaction, data access, and security services.

- Spring makes applications easier to test. Since components are POJOs, you can run them outside of any container. Because Spring uses important modern concepts such as aspect-oriented programming and dependency injections, coupling is looser. Because the container is fast and light, you can easily run it in integration tests.
- Spring helps remove dependencies from your code, decoupling it from its environment (such as an application server) and the Spring container itself. This protects your investment in your core intellectual property.

As the founder of the Spring project, I've been delighted to see the community grow from strength to strength. Books have played an important role in that progression, from the outset. This book is another important step in helping to bring Spring to a wider audience, and I'm delighted to see an author of Bruce's talent and reputation writing about Spring.

Bruce has always advocated simple, effective, pragmatic solutions, so it's not surprising that he was an early advocate of Spring. He's worked hard to promote the ideas behind Spring, teach it to customers, and win the hearts and minds of others in the industry. Following the bestselling *Better, Faster, Lighter Java*, this is the second book from his partnership with Justin Gehtland in which he's explained the value propostion and helped developers to benefit from it.

This is a valuable, timely, practical guide. It will help you start out with Spring and develop successful applications. Enjoy, and welcome to the Spring community!

—Rod Johnson
*CEO, Interface21*
*Founder, Spring Framework*
*London, March 2005*

# Preface

In 2004, Erik Hatcher traveled from a very wet Virginia to a usually dry Austin and got lucky. Barton Creek was up. Together, we braved the cold and windy conditions, and had one of the best kayaking days of our lives. In 2000, three friends and I drove east in March to run the Little River through the Great Smokey Mountains. As we put in, two inches of snow frosted the landscape, and flakes lightly dusted our boats on another memorable, incredible day, ripping through rapids like the Sinks (I walked around it) and the Elbow (I ran it, and didn't sleep for a week afterwards). The cold weather that starts a new paddling season adds an indescribable kind of energy to a run. There's just something magical about the thaw—the springtime.

In the Java community, we're encountering a Spring of a different kind. This one follows the great freeze of Enterprise JavaBeans 2.x (EJB). Tens of thousands of applications lay in frigid, near-death conditions in this well-intentioned, massive block of ice. EJB can suck the life right out of a developer if you're not careful, and sometimes, even if you are:

- Though developers use automated testing as a cornerstone practice, you can't test EJB applications well at all. The container is too big to start in a test case, and objects can't live outside of the container.

- EJB is incredibly intrusive. True, it's designed to shield your business objects from the details of transactions, persistence, security, remoting and messaging. It just does a terrible job. Your application becomes a slave to the EJB way.

- EJB forces unnatural design decisions. EJB applications must use dumbed-down value objects instead of rich domain objects. Like the Pied Piper, EJB capabilities like remoting entice developers to distribute applications in unsound ways. Limitations of EJB persistence force suboptimal designs, because they don't support critical concepts like inheritance.

And so, after years of plodding through monolithic EJB architectures and design patterns that are nothing more than workarounds for obvious problems, the whole enterprise Java community is ready for the Spring thaw. Rather than the large dominant vendors, a new breed of lightweight development processes and open source frameworks is supplying the heat.

Still, many developers resist change. To them, EJB is worth the pain, because of the value of declarative services like transactions and remoting. Breaking these ideas out of mainline business logic makes applications simpler, cleaner, and easier to maintain. But if declarative services are so important, why stop with just the declarative services provided by the container? Why not make a general model that makes it easy to attach services to any POJO?

In the end, I don't kayak and code for the same reasons. I kayak to have fun. I code to make money, and to get stuff done. If there's a good way to provide persistence (such as Hibernate or JDO) or transactions (such as JTA or JDBC), I should be able to tell the computer to make some *thing* transactional, or persistent, or remote, or secure.

In Spring, you can make an object secure, remote, or transactional with a couple of lines of XML. The resulting application is simple and clean. In Spring, you can work less and go home, because you can strip away a whole lot of the redundant code that you tend to see in most J2EE applications. You won't be nearly as burdened with meaningless detail. In Spring, you can often change your mind without the consequences bleeding through your entire application. You'll adapt much more quickly than you ever could before.

That's why I'm ready for the thaw.

## How to Use This Book

As with all books in the Developer's Notebook series, we're not going to pretend to give you a definitive reference. Instead, we hope to get you going quickly. You'll do so by getting your hands dirty. You'll work through one example after another. In the end, we hope you'll find the energy and promise of the Spring framework. Before you go too far, let me point you to the chapters that might be most interesting to you.

You can get the examples for this book, both in completed form and for each chapter and lab individually. Since Spring's such a wide-ranging project, you may want to skip a chapter here or there. I'm not going to restate the table of contents. In fact, most developer notebook readers probably skip the preface until the third or fourth reading anyway. Still, I should give you a couple of pointers that could save you some time.

- If you're interested in the basics of dependency injection, you'll want to pay close attention to Chapter 1.

- If you like to build user interfaces, you'll like Chapters 2, 3, and 9. If you're interested in Spring's proprietary way of doing things, check out Chapters 2 (WebMVC) and 9 (the Spring Rich sandbox project). Chapter 3 is dedicated to JSF and Struts.

- If you're into persistence, you'll like Chapters 4 and 5. Chapter 4 deals with JDBC, and Chapter 5 dives into true ORM solutions. Many people adopt Spring because it makes persistence so much easier.

- If you're hazy on AOP and how Spring's version works, you'll like Chapter 6, but if you don't plan to build your own services, you could easily skip it.

In short, look to this book for examples. Unlike examples in pure code form, these will talk to you. As I've read through examples, I've often wondered why some decisions were made. With this developer notebook, you'll have a running commentary. We hope you enjoy it.

## Conventions Used in This Book

The following typographical conventions are used in this book:

Plain text
> Indicates menu titles, menu options, menu buttons, and keyboard accelerators (such as Alt and Ctrl).

Italic
> Indicates new terms, URLs, email addresses, filenames, and file extensions.

Constant width
> Indicates extensions, pathnames, Unix utilities, commands, options, switches, variables, attributes, keys, functions, types, classes, namespaces, methods, modules, properties, parameters, values, objects, events, event handlers, XML tags, HTML tags, macros, the contents of files, or the output from commands.

```
Constant width bold
```
Shows commands or other text that should be typed literally by the user.

```
Constant width italic
```
Shows text that should be replaced with user-supplied values.

## Using Code Examples

This book is here to help you get your job done. In general, you may use the code in this book in your programs and documentation. You do not need to contact us for permission unless you're reproducing a significant portion of the code. For example, writing a program that uses several chunks of code from this book does not require permission. Selling or distributing a CD-ROM of examples from O'Reilly books *does* require permission. Answering a question by citing this book and quoting example code does not require permission. Incorporating a significant amount of example code from this book into your product's documentation *does* require permission.

We appreciate, but do not require, attribution. An attribution usually includes the title, author, publisher, and ISBN. For example: "*Spring: A Developer's Notebook*, by Bruce A. Tate and Justin Gehtland. Copyright 2005 O'Reilly Media, Inc., 0-596-00910-0."

## Comments and Questions

Please address comments and questions concerning this book to the publisher:

O'Reilly Media, Inc.
1005 Gravenstein Highway North
Sebastopol, CA 95472
(800) 998-9938 (in the United States or Canada)
(707) 829-0515 (international or local)
(707) 829-0104 (fax)

We have a web page for this book, where we list errata, examples, and any additional information. You can access this page at:

*http://www.oreilly.com/catalog/springadn*

To comment or ask technical questions about this book, send email to:

*bookquestions@oreilly.com*

For more information about our books, conferences, Resource Centers, and the O'Reilly Network, see our web site at:

*http://www.oreilly.com*

## Safari® Enabled

 When you see a Safari® Enabled icon on the cover of your favorite technology book, it means the book is available online through the O'Reilly Network Safari Bookshelf.

Safari offers a better solution than e-books. It's a virtual library that lets you easily search thousands of top technology books, cut and paste code samples, download chapters, and find quick answers when you need the most accurate, current information. Try it free at *http://safari.oreilly.com*.

## Collective Acknowledgments

There's more than a good author behind a good book, and this one is no exception. To be interesting, a Developer's Notebook needs a compelling technology, and Spring certainly fits that bill. Thanks to Rod Johnson and Juergen Hoeller, for meticulously breathing life into these ideas. We're in awe of what you've accomplished. Many of you probably bought the book because of another name on the cover, O'Reilly. That's no accident. Thanks to all of the supporting people who make it so. You'll find many of them in the back of this book, but we want to call a little more attention to a few of them.

Thanks to Kyle Hart, for your tireless promotion of this book, and of *Better, Faster, Lighter Java*. Thanks to Mike Loukides, both for your friendship, and for your guiding touch. You've got the sixth sense that all great editors have, and we genuinely appreciate the little time that we've spent together.

Good books also need good reviewers. Thanks to Mike's mystery reviewer, who provided the harsh, critical commentary that often wakes an author team up, and alerts them to danger. Thanks especially to David Rupp. We added you as an afterthought, and you turned out to be the best reviewer of the bunch. Even so, some mistakes could have escaped their tireless eyes. Those mistakes are ours, and not the reviewers.

We also would like to thank the gracious folks at JetBrains for a great IDE. It helped us write this book much more quickly than we otherwise would have. As always, we thank those Java users groups and events like JavaGruppen in Denmark, for giving us the opportunity to hone this message.

## Acknowledgments from Bruce

I'd like to thank Rod Johnson for friendship and opportunities. I wish you the best of luck with Interface 21. I thank Jay Zimmerman, for all you've done to help promote me and my books. I love your win–win style of business, even when I'm taking a three-stop flight to save you eight bucks. You've built a marvelous thing, and I'm glad that people are starting to recognize that. I'd also like to thank the many customers who treated me so well on the road, and looked over this book as it was under development—especially Trek and ProClarity. I hope you're able to put it into practice, and that it helps you do some great things.

Most authors wind up thanking their families, and there's a good reason for that. Family stirs the passion that it takes to write a good book. Family bears the brunt of the frustration and after-hours work that books always generate. I dare you to try to stay frustrated in the midst of little girl giggles. Thanks to Kayla and Julia for your laughter and smiles. Families encourage the best in us. Thanks to Maggie, my inspiration, for staying beside me and believing in me when others didn't, and for being there—even when I'm not. I love you more than you'll ever know.

## Acknowledgments from Justin

No technical work like this one exists in a vacuum; the decision to write a book is based on the imperative pressed on you by great new technologies that need to be talked about. As such, without Rod Johnson and Juergen Hoeller, I'd never have had the opportunity to write this book in the first place. Secondly, the book itself is shaped by the people you hang out with while writing it, so thanks to all the folks on the No Fluff tour, who make up 98% of my social life: Ted Neward, Dave Thomas, David Geary, Erik Hatcher, Dion Almaer, Jason Hunter, Nick Liesecki, Mike Clark, and of course, Jay Zimmerman. Each of you is an inspiration.

Thanks (again) to Stuart Halloway, a great business partner and even better influence. Your tireless dedication to learning new things, even if you forget them minutes later, is a compelling beacon.

Finally, I too have to thank my family. My daughter, Zoe, who is now learning to say all kinds of wonderful things like "car" and "house" and "protein" and "Cthulhu," proves to me every day that life is beautiful. And my wife, Lisa, who, through whatever twists and turns I throw at her, manages to say "That sounds like a great idea." Your tireless support and unconditional love keep me going.

# CHAPTER 1

# Getting Started

I'm a bona fide weekend extremist. I've done some pretty crazy things on a mountain bike, by layman's standards, and I love to kayak. I've been in serious trouble exactly once. I was on a river called the Piedra that I'd never run before, with new equipment and new techniques in my head. In kayaking, simplicity and speed are life, but I was tentative and slow. Instead of attacking the river, it attacked me, and I swam through three distinct class IV rapids, and was very lucky to emerge unscathed.

In software development, too, speed and simplicity are life. The *Spring framework* gives me both. Since you've bought this book, you likely agree. While it is simple, Spring also has power. Tremendous power. It will help you to layer and decouple your applications. You'll be able to test with a simplicity and clarity that you've not dreamed of before. In this chapter, you're going to take a simple application, automate it, and enable it for Spring.

## Building Two Classes with a Dependency

Many teachers and consultants write about dependencies like mayonnaise that's been left out in the sun too long, but if your application is to do anything interesting at all, it must have dependencies. The trick is to identify important dependencies, and deal with them in the right way. The way that you manage them will determine whether your application is easy to maintain, extend, and test. In this book, we'll do a mountain bike reservation system. A sports shop could use such a system for bike rentals. We'll start small, with all of the dependencies hardwired, to make sure that our infrastructure works. Then, we'll loosen the coupling

*In this chapter:*
- *Building Two Classes with a Dependency*
- *Using Dependency Injection*
- *Automating the Example*
- *Injecting Dependencies with Spring*
- *Writing a Test*

*Spring is the most popular of a new breed of so-called lightweight containers. When you add all of the supporting frameworks, Spring is fairly hefty, but "lightweight" refers to all of the crud that usually accompanies code that you put into the container.*

with Spring, and progressively add persistence, a web-based presentation layer, declarative transactions, and other services.

For me, Spring style development is iterative. The first couple of labs are all about ramping up our infrastructure slowly. The first example will make sure that we have a working Java environment, and it will start to build our core model. Each of the first few examples ramp up one small part of your environment, making it easy to troubleshoot anything that might go wrong.

## How do I do that?

Start with two classes in a single directory. One's a mountain bike, and the other is a registry that holds bikes. Call it a façade. You'll add bikes to the store within the façade constructor, and then print them all out using a third primitive class. (All of the classes shown in the book reside in a single package, com.springbook, unless otherwise specified.)

Example 1-1 shows the bike.

**Example 1-1.** Bike.java

```java
public class Bike {
    private String manufacturer;
    private String model;
    private int frame;
    private String serialNo;
    private double weight;
    private String status;

    public Bike(String manufacturer, String model, int frame,
                String serialNo, double weight, String status) {

        this.manufacturer = manufacturer;
        this.model = model;
        this.frame = frame;
        this.serialNo = serialNo;
        this.weight = weight;
        this.status = status;
    }

    public String toString() {
        return "Bike : " +
                "manufacturer -- " + manufacturer +
                "\n: model -- " + model +
                "\n: frame -- " + frame +
                "\n: serialNo -- " + serialNo +
                "\n: weight -- " + weight +
                "\n: status -- " + status +
                ".\n";
    }
}
```

**Example 1-1.** Bike.java (continued)

```
    public String getManufacturer() { return manufacturer; }

    public void setManufacturer(String manufacturer) {
        this.manufacturer = manufacturer;
    }

    public String getModel() { return model; }

    public void setModel(String model) { this.model = model; }

    public int getFrame() { return frame; }

    public void setFrame(int frame) { this.frame = frame; }

    public String getSerialNo() { return serialNo; }

    public void setSerialNo(String serialNo) { this.serialNo = serialNo; }

    public double getWeight() { return weight; }

    public void setWeight(double weight) { this.weight = weight; }

    public String getStatus() { return status; }

    public void setStatus(String status) { this.status = status; }
}
```

Example 1-2 is the façade.

**Example 1-2.** RentABike.java

```
import java.util.*;
public class RentABike {

    private String storeName;
    final List bikes = new ArrayList();

    public RentABike(String storeName) {
        this.storeName = storeName;
        bikes.add(new Bike("Shimano", "Roadmaster", 20, "11111", 15,
                        "Fair"));
        bikes.add(new Bike("Cannondale", "F2000 XTR", 18, "22222",12,
                        "Excellent"));
        bikes.add(new Bike("Trek","6000", 19, "33333", 12.4,
                        "Fair"));
    }

    public String toString() { return "RentABike: " + storeName; }

    public List getBikes() { return bikes; }

    public Bike getBike(String serialNo) {
        Iterator iter = bikes.iterator();
        while(iter.hasNext()) {
```

**Example 1-2.** RentABike.java (continued)

```
            Bike bike = (Bike)iter.next();
            if(serialNo.equals(bike.getSerialNo())) return bike;
        }
        return null;
    }
}
```

Finally, Example 1-3 is the view.

**Example 1-3.** CommandLineView.java

```
import java.util.*;
public class CommandLineView {
    private RentABike rentaBike;
    public CommandLineView() {rentaBike = new RentABike("Bruce's Bikes"); }

    public void printAllBikes() {
        System.out.println(rentaBike.toString());
        Iterator iter = rentaBike.getBikes().iterator();
        while(iter.hasNext()) {
            Bike bike = (Bike)iter.next();
            System.out.println(bike.toString());
        }
    }

    public static final void main(String[] args) {
        CommandLineView clv = new CommandLineView();
        clv.printAllBikes();
    }
}
```

*RentABike is a dependency. Using this style of programming, dependencies are hardcoded, increasing the coupling between the façade and the view. Spring will help to eliminate these kinds of dependencies.*

Next, you'll compile the application, like this:

```
C:\RentABikeApp\src> javac -d ../out *.java
```

Your output directory now contains the compiled class files.

```
Directory of C:\RentABikeApp\out

07/28/2004  10:12 AM    <DIR>          .
07/28/2004  10:12 AM    <DIR>          ..
07/28/2004  10:10 AM             1,753 Bike.class
07/28/2004  10:10 AM             1,431 RentABike.class
07/28/2004  10:10 AM               940 CommandLineView.class
```

Run the application like this:

```
C:\RentABikeApp\out> java CommandLineView

RentABike: Bruce's Bikes
Bike : manufacturer -- Shimano
: model -- Roadmaster
: frame -- 20
: serialNo -- 11111
: weight -- 15.0
: status -- Fair.
```

```
Bike : manufacturer -- Cannondale
     : model -- F2000 XTR
     : frame -- 18
     : serialNo -- 22222
     : weight -- 12.0
     : status -- Excellent.

Bike : manufacturer -- Trek
     : model -- 6000
     : frame -- 19
     : serialNo -- 33333
     : weight -- 12.4
     : status -- Fair.
```

## What just happened?

Nothing good. The current design is simple, but it's also hardwired. You can immediately see several problems:

- The façade layer (RentABike) statically creates the bikes in the store, so whenever any new bike comes in (yeah!) or a customer totals one on the mountain (boo!), you've got a code change.
- This model will also be difficult to test, because the set of bikes is fixed.
- The user interface and the façade are tightly coupled. You see a hard-coded dependency between the façade layer and the user interface.
- The code base is not organized, and the build is not automated.

But we're willing to take some short cuts to get the Java base working, and the underpinnings of the application under way. We'll decouple and automate in the next example.

*The fundamental design pattern in Spring, and all other lightweight containers, is based on the idea of loosening coupling between dependencies.*

## What about...

...rolling up the whole burrito all at once? You might decide to install Spring, Hibernate, Java, Ant, and JUnit all at the same time. It's been my experience that if you control one variable at a time, you actually save time, especially as you're establishing your foundation. Once you've got all of your tools installed and working, then you can collect many of these steps into one.

# Using Dependency Injection

When I begin to build any application, it's usually tightly coupled. That's okay. I can always refactor it later. In this example, I'll structure the application so that it will work with Spring when I add it. I introduce an interface to the façade layer, so that I can have a façade layer that implements several different strategies.

The first step to learning Spring is the *dependency injection* pattern. It's not complicated, but it's the central concept. It's different enough from the typical way that most people code that you'll want to get it down quickly.

Figure 1-1 shows a client and server prepared for dependency injection. A client uses another class that we'll call a *service*. The client has a property that accepts a service. The service is wrapped in an interface. The client can't see the implementation of the service. But this code is not yet loosely coupled: you still have to create the service somewhere. With dependency injection, a third-party, called the *assembler* or *container*, creates both the client and service, and then sets the value of aService (which is a reference to an instance of Service) to satisfy the dependency.

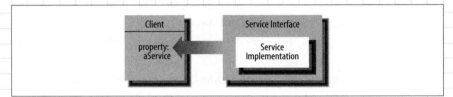

**Figure 1-1.** This client uses a service wrapped in an interface

You probably already code this way in spots. You'll see how powerful this programming model can be when you use it in a framework that applies it in a consistent way across your application. Code made of decoupled components is easier to test, maintain, and understand.

## How do I do that?

You don't have to use a lightweight container to use this design pattern. To decouple with dependency injection, there are three steps:

1. Wrap the service in an interface.

2. Add a property to the client, to refer to the service.

3. With a third party framework or custom code, build the service and populate the property.

The first step is to extract the interface. We'll rename the RentABike file, class definition, and constructor to ArrayListRentABike (Example 1-4), and create an interface (Example 1-5).

*Many see dependency injection for the first time and wonder, "What's the big deal?" After working with it some, they come to understand that this simple change can dramatically improve their code and ease future maintenance.*

**Example 1-4.** ArrayListRentABike.java (renamed from RentABike.java)

```java
import java.util.*;

public class ArrayListRentABike implements RentABike {
    private String storeName;
    final List bikes = new ArrayList();

    public ArrayListRentABike() { initBikes(); }

    public ArrayListRentABike(String storeName) {
        this.storeName = storeName;
        initBikes();
    }

    public void initBikes() {
        bikes.add(new Bike("Shimano", "Roadmaster", 20, "11111", 15, "Fair"));
        bikes.add(new Bike("Cannondale", "F2000 XTR", 18, "22222", 12,
                "Excellent"));
        bikes.add(new Bike("Trek", "6000", 19, "33333", 12.4, "Fair"));
    }

    public String toString() { return "RentABike: " + storeName; }

    public List getBikes() { return bikes; }

    public Bike getBike(String serialNo) {
        Iterator iter = bikes.iterator();
        while(iter.hasNext()) {
            Bike bike = (Bike)iter.next();
            if(serialNo.equals(bike.getSerialNo())) return bike;
        }
        return null;
    }
}
```

**Example 1-5.** RentABike.java

```java
import java.util.*;
interface RentABike {
    List getBikes();
    Bike getBike(String serialNo);
}
```

Next, Example 1-6 gives the view. Note that we've extracted the methods that print out the bikes to the command line. We also add a property to the view, which uses the RentABike interface.

**Example 1-6.** CommandLineView.java

```java
import java.util.*;
public class CommandLineView {
    private RentABike rentaBike;
```

*Here, you see the RentABike service exposed as a property. It will later be populated by Spring.*

**Example 1-6.** CommandLineView.java (continued)

```java
public CommandLineView( ) { }

public void setRentaBike(RentABike rentaBike) {
    this.rentaBike = rentaBike;
}

public RentABike getRentaBike( ) { return this.rentaBike;}

public void printAllBikes() {
    System.out.println(rentaBike.toString( ));
    Iterator iter = rentaBike.getBikes().iterator( );
    while(iter.hasNext( )) {
        Bike bike = (Bike)iter.next( );
        System.out.println(bike.toString( ));
    }
}
}
```

Finally, we have an assembler that creates each object, and sets the property (Example 1-7).

*You can see the dependency injection happening here. Third-party code—custom code in this case—creates both objects, and injects the value of RentABike into the view.*

**Example 1-7.** RentABikeAssembler.java

```java
public class RentABikeAssembler {
    public static final void main(String[] args) {
        CommandLineView clv = new CommandLineView( );
        RentABike rentaBike = new ArrayListRentABike("Bruce's Bikes");
        clv.setRentaBike(rentaBike);
        clv.printAllBikes( );
    }
}
```

Next, you'll compile the application like this:

```
C:\RentABikeApp\src> javac -d ../out *.java
```

Your output directory now contains the compiled class files.

```
Directory of C:\RentABikeApp\out

07/28/2004  10:12 AM    <DIR>          .
07/28/2004  10:12 AM    <DIR>          ..
07/28/2004  10:50 AM             1,475 ArrayListRentABike.class
07/28/2004  10:50 AM             1,753 Bike.class
07/28/2004  10:50 AM               186 RentABike.class
07/28/2004  10:50 AM               495 RentABikeAssembler.class
07/28/2004  10:50 AM               944 CommandLineView.class
```

Run the application like this:

```
C:\RentABikeApp\out>java RentABikeAssembler

RentABike: Bruce's Bikes
Bike : manufacturer -- Shimano
```

```
: model -- Roadmaster
: frame -- 20
: serialNo -- 11111
: weight -- 15.0
: status -- Fair.

Bike : manufacturer -- Cannondale
: model -- F2000 XTR
: frame -- 18
: serialNo -- 22222
: weight -- 12.0
: status -- Excellent.

Bike : manufacturer -- Trek
: model -- 6000
: frame -- 19
: serialNo -- 33333
: weight -- 12.4
: status -- Fair.
```

## What just happened?

You just saw an example of dependency injection, outside of a light-weight container. The lightweight container community makes a whole lot of noise, but the ideas behind the movement are simple. Program using interfaces, and let a third party inject the dependency instead of setting it yourself.

You're going to eventually replace the assembler with Spring. When that happens, Spring will actually fire the constructors for our objects and set the dependencies. But first, you'll need to give this build a little attention.

## What about...

...service locators, or factory objects? Of course, dependency injection is not the only way to manage dependencies. In fact, it's not the only good way. J2EE users tend to use service locators. Using that pattern (shown in Figure 1-2), you take a dependency, wrap it in an interface, register it in a dictionary, and then look it up using a helper class called a locator. It's not a bad approach.

The dependency injection strategy lets you pick a consistent approach, and separate the dependency completely from your application. You'll see how this approach will help you test, and help you build applications that are easy to customize and configure.

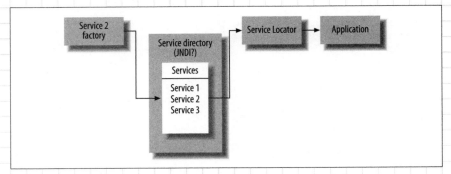

**Figure 1-2.** J2EE applications manage dependencies with service locators

In fact, earlier lightweight containers, like Avalon, used this approach. Most modern containers provide dependency lookup, but prefer other types of dependency resolution.

# Automating the Example

It's time for a little housekeeping. To go much further, you need to automate. You probably already use Ant. It's a standardized way to organize all of the tasks that you need to build your application. If you don't already use it, you need to.

Ant has become ubiquitous. In order to work with Java tools, you need to be able to speak the language. We're not going to provide yet another justification for Ant in this chapter, since you've probably read enough of them already.

## How do I do that?

You'll need to download an Ant distribution. You may as well use the one that comes with Spring (*http://springframework.org/*). To run all of the examples for this book, you'll want to get Spring version 1.1, or later. Follow all of the directions for your platform.

Next, you'll organize the directory structure in a way that's friendly for web applications and Spring. I recommend that you use the organization that you'll find with the Spring sample applications, so that you'll have a working example. These are the directories that you'll use:

*src*

> This directory has the home for all of the source code in your application. As usual, you'll want the directory structure to mirror your package structure.

*test*

> This directory has the home for all of your unit tests. We'll talk more about JUnit in the last lab.

*db*

> This directory has the home for all database specific scripts, configuration, and code. Some of these will be configuration files, some will help set up a database with the correct schema, and some will help initialize the database with test data, if necessary. If you support multiple databases, each will have its own directory under *db*.

*war*

> The *war* file is the typical deployable unit for the web application. If you're using a J2EE web container or a servlet container like Tomcat, the web.xml configuration file will go here. Spring's configuration files will also go here. We'll talk more about Spring's configuration files as we layer on additional labs.

To start with, place the source files like this:

- *RentABike.java* goes in *src*, in the correct package hierarchy.
- *ArrayListRentABike* goes in *src*, with *RentABike*.
- *Bike* goes in *src*, with *RentABike*.
- *CommandLineView* goes in *src*, with *RentABike*.

Finally, you'll need an Ant build script, which we'll place in the root folder of our project. Example 1-8 is the one that we'll use to start with.

**Example 1-8.** build.xml

```
<?xml version="1.0"?>
<project name="RentABike" default="compile" basedir=".">

    <property name="src.dir" value="src"/>
    <property name="test.dir" value="test"/>
    <property name="war.dir" value="war"/>
    <property name="class.dir" value="${war.dir}/classes"/>

    <target name="init">
        <mkdir dir="${class.dir}"/>
    </target>

    <target name="compile" depends="init"
            description="Compiles all source code">
        <javac srcdir="${src.dir}"
               destdir="${class.dir}"
        />
    </target>
```

*Here's where you'll tell Ant where the class files are for a given application. You can ship these with your war file, or you can point them directly to their installations, and tell your users which files they need to deploy.*

**Example 1-8.** build.xml (continued)

```
<target name="clean" description="Erases contents of classes dir">
    <delete dir="${class.dir}"/>
</target>

</project>
```

To run a build, switch to the directory called C:\RentABikeApp> and type:

```
[1]C:\RentABikeApp>ant
Buildfile: build.xml

init:
    [mkdir] Created dir: C:\RentABikeApp\war\WEB-INF\classes

compile:
    [javac] Compiling 5 source files to C:\RentABikeApp\war\WEB-INF\classes

BUILD SUCCESSFUL
Total time: 2 seconds
```

*That's what I call automation. We've reduced the total keystrokes that you'll need to build the project to four.*

## What just happened?

Ant built the system in one automated step. That's not such a big deal now, but it will be increasingly important as the build steps get more sophisticated. You'll want the system to run unit tests, add any precompilation steps such as JDO's byte code enhancement in Chapter 5, or copy configuration files to the appropriate place. You can also have special tasks to initialize a database or deploy our war file to an application server.

## What about...

*Actually, we're developing this application in the IDE called IDEA, made by JetBrains. We find that it has the best refactoring support out there. Take heart. We also test the Ant version of each lab.*

...the fact that some integrated development environments don't need Ant at all? If you want to work with these without Ant, you'll need to make sure that:

- You structure the code in the same directories that we do, so that packages will line up correctly.
- You make sure that your IDE can reach all of the *.lib* files that we tell you to use.
- In future chapters, you'll need to worry about how to deploy and run a web application, and how to run JUnit.

From here on out, we'll tell you when you need to add a new directory, execute the application, or make a new library available. We won't tell you how. We assume you know how to use your own IDE, or Ant directly.

# Injecting Dependencies with Spring

You're almost through with the setup for Spring. It's time to download it and put it into action. In this lab, you'll replace the RentABikeAssembler object with Spring.

When I started using Spring instead of J2EE, it changed my life. I got more productive. My code got easier for me to write, and easier for my customers to understand. Since it was simpler, it often executed faster. It was also infinitely easier to refactor. In fact, I wrote a book about the value of lightweight frameworks like Spring, called *Better, Faster, Lighter Java* (O'Reilly).

## How do I do that?

You'll first have to download Spring. Go get it at *http://www.springframework.org*. That will point you to sourceforge, where you'll get the best version for your platform. We used Version 1.1. You will need to add a new folder to your project, *war\WEB-INF\lib*, and put the Spring libraries there (everything in the *\dist* folder of your Spring distribution).

Moving a well-designed plain-ordinary-Java-object (POJO) application to Spring is straightforward. It only takes three steps:

- Refactor your code to take advantage of dependency injection. Model objects are beans, and services are aspects. Usually, you'll only have beans.
- Remove the code that instantiates the objects and sets dependencies.
- Build a configuration file describing your beans and aspects.
- Access your code through Spring.

Since our individual parts are already built to take advantage of dependency injection, moving to Spring is an easy exercise. We simply replace our assembler with a Spring version, and provide a configuration file which will go in the *\war\WEB-INF* folder.

Example 1-9 shows the configuration file.

**Example 1-9.** RentABike-context.xml

```
<?xml version="1.0" encoding="UTF-8"?>
<!DOCTYPE beans PUBLIC "-//SPRING//DTD BEAN//EN" "http://www.springframework.org/
dtd/spring-beans.dtd">
```

**Example 1-9.** RentABike-context.xml (continued)

```xml
<beans>

    <bean id="rentaBike" class="ArrayListRentABike">
        <property name="storeName"><value>"Bruce's Bikes"</value></property>
    </bean>

    <bean id="commandLineView" class="CommandLineView">
        <property name="rentaBike"><ref bean="rentaBike"/></property>
    </bean>

</beans>
```

And Example 1-10 is the new assembler that replaced the old RentABikeAssembler.

**Example 1-10.** RentABikeAssembler.java

```java
import org.springframework.context.support.ClassPathXmlApplicationContext;

public class RentABikeAssembler {
    public static final void main(String[] args) {
        ClassPathXmlApplicationContext ctx = new
            ClassPathXmlApplicationContext("RentABikeApp-context.xml");
        CommandLineView clv =
            (CommandLineView)ctx.getBean("commandLineView");
        clv.printAllBikes();
    }
}
```

# What just happened?

You may be scratching your head and wondering what the big deal is all about. These tiny improvements in architecture will have profound implications throughout the lifecycle of this application. You'll see the benefits almost immediately. I won't harp on them here. Instead, let's talk about what's happening under the covers.

# What about...

...Pico, Hive Mind, and Avalon? These are all lightweight containers. Each of them has strengths and weaknesses. Neither Avalon nor Hive Mind have the critical mass that you'll want out of a container, especially if you want services that interoperate. Right now, Spring and Pico have the most market share. People tend to use Pico if they want a standalone container, but Spring has the most comprehensive support for additional services, such as declarative transactions and a rich persistence strategy.

# Writing a Test

We'll finish each chapter with a test. In fact, if you're a true believer in test-driven development, you should code your test cases *first*. Many of you bought this book because Spring can improve the testability of your applications. In fact, improving testability was one of the fundamental drivers of Spring's architecture from the beginning.

Automating your tests gives you more confidence that your code will work right, and will keep working right as you make changes. In fact, our managers are all reading the same books that say that it's expensive to keep large testing organizations in place. We've got to pick up the slack. There's no effective way to do that without automation. There's a big problem, though. Many of our current development architectures, like EJB and Struts, do not support testing very well. They're expensive to load, and hard to mock.

Spring changes all of that. Each object can run outside of the container. Further, since the container itself is so light, the startup cost is negligible. That's a huge win for you, if you want to test. Finally, Spring encourages designs with very loose coupling between components.

## How do I do that?

Think of a unit test as another client of your application. The test makes assertions about what should be true should the application be working correctly. For example, if you add an object to a list, the size should increase by one. Then, you can run the test standalone while you're building a new feature or debugging an old one. You can also run the tests as part of the overall build. If the tests fail, then the build fails.

Each test case is a subclass of TestCase. In Example 1-11, the test will be a client of the façade.

**Example 1-11.** RentABikeTest.java

```java
public class RentABikeTest extends TestCase{

    private RentABike rentaBike;

    public void setUp() {
        rentaBike = new ArrayListRentABike("Bruce's Bikes");
    }

    public void testGetName() {
        assertEquals("Bruce's Bikes", rentaBike.getStoreName());
    }
```

**Example 1-11.** RentABikeTest.java (continued)

```java
    public void testGetBike( ) {
        Bike bike = rentaBike.getBike("11111");
        assertNotNull(bike);
        assertEquals("Shimano", bike.getManufacturer( ));
    }

    public void testGetBikes( ) {
        List bikes = rentaBike.getBikes( );
        assertNotNull(bikes);
        assertEquals(3, bikes.size( ));
    }
}
```

Next, you'll need to modify Ant to run the tests. Example 1-12 gives the additional task to compile the test (note that you'll have to modify PATH_TO_JUNIT to be appropriate for your environment).

**Example 1-12.** build.xml

```xml
<property name="test.class.dir" value="${test.dir}/classes"/>
<path id="bikestore.class.path">
    <fileset dir="${spring.dir}/dist">
        <include name="*.jar"/>
    </fileset>
    <pathelement location="${spring.dir}/lib/jakarta-commons
            /commons-logging.jar"/>
    <pathelement location="${spring.dir}/lib/log4j/log4j-1.2.8.jar"/>
    <pathelement location="${spring.dir}/lib/j2ee/servlet.jar"/>
    <dirset dir="${basedir}"/>
    <dirset dir="${class.dir}"/>
</path>
<path id="junit.class.path">
    <path refid="bikestore.class.path"/>
    <pathelement location="PATH_TO_JUNIT"/>
</path>
<target name="compile.test" depends="init"
        description="Compiles all unit test source">
    <javac srcdir="${test.dir}"
        destdir="${test.class.dir}"
        classpathref="junit.class.path"/>
</target>
```

Example 1-13 is the task to run the tests.

**Example 1-13.** build.xml

```xml
<target name="test" depends="compile.test, compile"
        description="Runs the unit tests">
    <junit printsummary="withOutAndErr" haltonfailure="no"
            haltonerror="no" fork="yes">
        <classpath refid="junit.class.path"/>
```

**Example 1-13.** build.xml (continued)

```
            <formatter type="xml" usefile="true" />
            <batchtest todir="${test.dir}">
                <fileset dir="${test.class.dir}">
                    <include name="*Test.*"/>
                </fileset>
            </batchtest>
        </junit>
    </target>
</target>
```

Here's the result of the test:

```
Buildfile: build.xml

init:

compile:

compile.test:

test:
    [junit] Running RentABikeTest
    [junit] Tests run: 3, Failures: 0, Errors: 0, Time elapsed: 0.36 sec

BUILD SUCCESSFUL
Total time: 2 seconds
```

# What just happened?

Ant just built the entire application, including the tests. Then, Ant ran the tests. All succeeded. If a test case had failed, then you'd have to make it pass before the build could be successful. In this way, you catch small errors before they become larger ones.

In the next chapter, we'll really start to exercise Spring. We'll build a true user interface for this application using Spring's WebMVC. We'll also show you how to integrate existing user interface components into Spring.

# CHAPTER 2

# Building a User Interface

I was hauling down a trail called Emma Long, and came up to a four-foot drop. In a split second, I had to make the decision of whether to jump the ledge, try to ride down it, or stop and get off my bike. I once read that in Austin, Texas, there are more broken mountain bike frames than any other place, per capita. Though I've never confirmed it, I believe it, because there are so many rocky trails with ledges that are small enough to handle *sometimes* with a cheap bike, but also big enough to snap the frame. Web-based user interface development is similar. It's easy to get started down that trail with a bike that's not quite up to the task. Often, it's the framework and organization of the code that's just *behind* the user interface that presents the biggest problem. In this chapter, you'll learn how Spring can help. We'll focus on Spring's Web MVC framework, but in the next chapter, we'll also show you how to integrate alternative frameworks, and even use rich clients.

*Spring doesn't force you to use a full application server. Actually, you don't even have to build web-based applications. The requirement for Tomcat is really a requirement for some servlet container, purely because this application (not Spring) requires it.*

## Setting Up Tomcat

In this first example, you'll learn how to build a simple user interface with Tomcat with Spring's *Web MVC* framework. You'll add a couple of screens to add bikes to the inventory of rental bikes. Then, we'll add a hardwired JSP that will let you add a new bike to the database.

Spring doesn't give you a servlet container. Instead, it just gives you a set of services that make it easier to build web applications.

Most projects simply don't need a full-blown J2EE container. One of the best things about Spring is that you can deploy it, in production, without paying for an application server, or the hardware that you'd need to run one. Tomcat will manage your servlets, provide an easy architecture for managing deployments, and let you manage its threading model.

# How do I do that?

First, you'll go to *http://jakarta.apache.org/tomcat*. There, you'll find
Apache Tomcat 5.0.27, which is the version that we're using for all of
our examples. If you want to use something else, that's okay. You'll just
need some type of servlet container that supports:

- JSP Version 1.2 or higher
- Servlet Version 2.3 or higher

Next, you'll modify the façade to the RentABike, so that you can do simple create/read/update/delete (CRUD) methods. Example 2-1 gives the
new façade.

**Example 2-1.** RentABike.java

```
public interface RentABike {
    List getBikes();
    Bike getBike(String serialNo);
    void saveBike(Bike bike);
    void deleteBike(Bike bike);
    void setStoreName(String name);
    String getStoreName();
}
```

*Here's the interface for the RentABike façade. You'll later see this injected with Spring.*

And you'll want to access that through a simple user interface. For now,
you'll hardwire the façade to a simple JSP. We'll do one simple JSP right
now, that outputs a list of all the bikes in the store (Example 2-2). Notice
that from here on out, we've moved our code into a package, *com.
springbook*. The source files for the domain classes should move into the
*src\com\springbook* folder as well. Here's the hardwired JSP.

**Example 2-2.** Listbikes.jsp

```
<%@ page import="com.springbook.*"%>
<% RentABike store = new ArrayListRentABike
                    ("Bruce's Bikes"); %>
<html>
    <head>
        <title>
            <%= store.getStoreName() %>
        </title>
    </head>
    <body>
        <h1><%= store.getStoreName() %></h1>
        <table border="1" cellspacing="2" cellpadding="2">
            <tr style="font-weight:bold">
                <td>Manufacturer</td><td>Model</td><td>Status</td>
            </tr>
            <% for(int i=0;i<store.getBikes().size();i++) { %>
```

**Example 2-2.** Listbikes.jsp (continued)

```
        <% Bike bike = (Bike)store.getBikes().get(i); %>
        <tr>
            <td><%= bike.getManufacturer() %></td>
            <td><%= bike.getModel() %></td>
            <td><%= bike.getStatus() %></td>
        </tr>
    <% } %>
  </table>
 </body>
</html>
```

Next, you'll want to configure the application. With J2EE servlets, that happens in the web.xml file. At this point, the web.xml file is simplicity itself. In fact, you could even leave it out for now, but for the sake of completeness, go ahead and add it. Example 2-3 shows the web.xml, which you'll put in a directory called war/WEB-INF, off of your main project directory.

**Example 2-3.** web.xml

```
<!DOCTYPE web-app
    PUBLIC  "-//Sun Microsystems, Inc.//DTD Web Application 2.2//EN"
    "http://java.sun.com/j2ee/dtds/web-app_2_2.dtd">
<web-app>
</web-app>
```

You'll need to change Ant's build.xml to add a deploy step. This step packages everything that Tomcat will need to run your application, including JSPs, Java classes, the servlet configuration in web.xml, and the Spring context. Example 2-4 gives the additions to the Ant script.

**Example 2-4.** build.xml

```
<property name="webapp.dir" value="C:/tomcat/webapps/bikestore"/>
<target name="deploy" depends="compile"
        description="Copies the contents of web-app to destination dir">
    <copy todir="${webapp.dir}">
        <fileset dir="${war.dir}"/>
    </copy>
</target>
```

Finally, you'll build and deploy, as in Example 2-5.

**Example 2-5.** Output from running Ant on build.xml

```
buildfile: build.xml

init:
    [mkdir] Created dir: C:\RentABikeApp\war\WEB-INF\classes
    [mkdir] Created dir: C:\RentABikeApp\test\classes
```

**Chapter 2: Building a User Interface**

**Example 2-5.** Output from running Ant on build.xml (continued)

```
compile:
    [javac] Compiling 9 source files to C:\RentABikeApp\war\WEB-INF\classes

deploy:
     [copy] Copying 9 files to C:\@Tools\Apache Software Foundation\Tomcat 5.0\
webapps\bikestore

BUILD SUCCESSFUL
Total time: 2 seconds
```

# What just happened?

You just walked through the build and deploy cycle for Tomcat, which is:

- Write the code for your application
- Configure it through web.xml
- Package it in a .war file
- Deploy it in Tomcat
- Run it

The browser makes a request to Tomcat, which then routes the request to a JSP. The first time that you run the application, Tomcat compiles the JSP into a servlet, and executes it. The JSP returns a result in the form of HTML, via HTTP, to the browser.

Of course, most J2EE applications have long since moved on to architectures like EJB that require much more than Tomcat. That's unfortunate, because many applications run just fine in a basic servlet container.

In fact, I've seen a resurgence of applications that put the full J2EE on the back burner, and choose to run simple containers. In my classes, I regularly ask how many people are using EJB, a full J2EE server without EJB, or a servlet container. The numbers of people choosing Tomcat, or something similar, is growing rapidly. Everything old is new again.

# Building a View with Web MVC

In this example, you'll build a simple web-based user interface with Spring's Web MVC framework. You'll use the code that you've accumulated for RentABike for the business logic, you'll use Spring to help you organize and configure the application, and you'll deploy it on Tomcat.

If you've done this for any length of time, you probably recognize that you're barreling down a trail that will break your frame if you're not careful. This simple application is not the ideal structure for a web

*Actually, the package step at this point is optional. You don't have to build a war; you can leave the files exploded. Most developers will eventually choose to do so.*

application. Changes in the application will trickle through the view, and changes in the view will require significant updates to your models. Experience has shown that it's better to have a model, view, and controller layer, with a variation of the model/view/controller (MVC) design pattern called *model2*, shown in Figure 2-1. This is the design that you'll be using in Spring's Web MVC, or most other MVC frameworks.

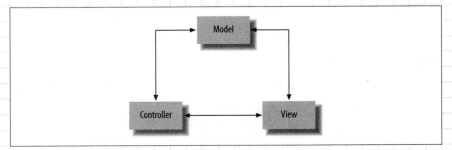

**Figure 2-1.** It's best to separate web applications into three distinct components: model, view, and controller

## How do I do that?

Like Struts, Web MVC lets you build applications with three distinct layers: the model, view, and controller. You'll also need to configure what you've done. Since you've already developed the model with the business logic (you'll specify the façade as your model), you're free to first concentrate on the view.

### The JSPs

For now, the view will be a thin JSP layer that lets you pick a bike from a list, then remove or edit it. You'll use another screen to add or edit bike information. We aren't focusing on formatting, since we're primarily interested in Spring's role. You'll use standard JSTL (available at *http://java.sun.com/products/jsp/jstl/*, or packaged with Spring). Add *standard.jar*, *jstl.jar*, *c.tld* and *fmt.tld* to your *war\WEB-INF\lib* folder. You'll link them through an *include.jsp* page which contains just the following two lines:

```
<%@ taglib prefix="c" uri="http://java.sun.com/jstl/core" %>
<%@ taglib prefix="fmt" uri="http://java.sun.com/jstl/fmt" %>
```

**Example 2-6.** bikes.jsp

```
<%@ page import="com.springbook.*"%>
<%@ include file="include.jsp" %>
```

**Example 2-6.** bikes.jsp (continued)

```html
<html>
   <head>
      <title>
         <c:out value="${rentaBike.storeName}"/>
      </title>
   </head>
   <body>
      <h1><c:out value="${rentaBike.storeName}"/></h1>
      Edit a bike: <br/>
      <c:forEach items="${rentaBike.bikes}" var="bike">
         <a href="editBike.bikes?bikeSerialNo=<c:out
            value="${bike.serialNo}"/>">
         <c:out value="${bike.manufacturer}"/> -
         <c:out value="${bike.model}"/><br/>
      </c:forEach>
      <br/><br/>
      <a href="newBike.bikes">Add a new bike</a>
   </body>
</html>
```

*The lines in bold are standard JSTL tags. You get a much cleaner syntax for outputting a simple JSP variable, or iterating through a list of items.*

This page will have a reference to an instance of RentABike to query for values. The JSTL tags <c:out> and <c:forEach> are used to query the properties of the RentABike implementation.

Example 2-7 is the JSP that adds a new entry or edits an old one.

**Example 2-7.** editBike.jsp

```html
<%@ page import="com.springbook.*"%>
<%@ include file="include.jsp" %>
<html>
   <head>
      <title>
         Edit Bike
      </title>
   </head>
   <body>
      <h1>Edit Bike</h1>
      <form method="POST" action="submitBike.bikes">
         <table border="1" cellspacing="2" cellpadding="2">
            <tr>
               <td align="right">Manufacturer:</td>
               <td>
                  <input type="text" name="manufacturer"
                     value="<c:out value="${bike.manufacturer}"/>">
               </td>
            </tr>
            <tr>
               <td align="right">Model:</td>
               <td>
                  <input type="text" name="model"
                     value="<c:out value="${bike.model}"/>">
```

**Example 2-7.** editBike.jsp (continued)

```
                </td>
            </tr>
            <tr>
                <td align="right">Frame:</td>
                <td>
                    <input type="text" name="frame"
                        value="<c:out value="${bike.frame}"/>">
                </td>
            </tr>
            <tr>
                <td align="right">Serial Number:</td>
                <td>
                    <input type="text" name="serialno"
                        value="<c:out value="${bike.serialNo}"/>">
                </td>
            </tr>
            <tr>
                <td align="right">Weight:</td>
                <td>
                    <input type="text" name="weight"
                        value="<c:out value="${bike.weight}"/>">
                </td>
            </tr>
            <tr>
                <td align="right">Status:</td>
                <td>
                    <input type="text" name="status"
                        value="<c:out value="${bike.status}"/>">
                </td>
            </tr>
        </table>
        <input type="submit" value="Submit">
    </form>
  </body>
</html>
```

Once again, you can use the standard <c:out> JSTL tags to output properties from an object, this time a Bike. If the Bike reference is empty, the tags will output the empty string, not throw an exception, which is precisely what you want. This way, if the page receives a Bike to edit, the fields will be filled in appropriately, and if it is used to add a *new* bike, then the fields will be empty when rendered.

## The controllers

For Web MVC, you'll have one controller for every screen. Each controller will return a model and view combination. It's customary to use a façade layer as your model. First, Example 2-8 gives the controller that lets you choose a bike.

**Example 2-8.** BikesController.java

```java
package com.springbook;
import org.springframework.web.servlet.mvc.Controller;
import org.springframework.web.servlet.ModelAndView;
import javax.servlet.http.HttpServletResponse;
import javax.servlet.http.HttpServletRequest;

public class BikesController implements Controller {
    private RentABike facade;
    public RentABike getFacade() { return facade;}

    public void setFacade(RentABike facade) { this.facade = facade; }

    public ModelAndView handleRequest(HttpServletRequest request,
        HttpServletResponse response) throws Exception {

        return new ModelAndView("bikes.jsp", "rentaBike", facade);
    }
}
```

*The controller will use the RentABike interface to manipulate any business logic. You'll later use Spring to inject this value.*

This controller merely forwards the user to the bikes.jsp page and hands a reference to the RentABike implementation provided by Spring. Next, Example 2-9 shows the controller that lets you add or edit a bike.

**Example 2-9.** EditBikeController.java

```java
package com.springbook;
import org.springframework.web.servlet.mvc.Controller;
import org.springframework.web.servlet.ModelAndView;
import javax.servlet.http.HttpServletRequest;
import javax.servlet.http.HttpServletResponse;

public class EditBikeController implements Controller {
    private RentABike facade;

    public RentABike getFacade() { return facade; }

    public void setFacade(RentABike facade) { this.facade = facade; }

    public ModelAndView handleRequest(HttpServletRequest request,
        HttpServletResponse response) throws Exception {

        if(request.getParameter("bikeSerialNo") == null) {
            System.out.println("bikeSerialNo was null");
            return new ModelAndView("editBike.jsp");
        } else {
            System.out.println("bikeSerialNo == " +
                request.getParameter("bikeSerialNo"));
            Bike bike =
                facade.getBike(request.getParameter("bikeSerialNo"));
            return new ModelAndView("editBike.jsp", "bike", bike);
        }
    }
}
```

*This class looks like it uses a servlet interface. It doesn't. Unlike controllers from Struts, Spring controllers implement an interface. This design makes it easer test with a technique called mocking.*

*The controller does a little error-checking, and then uses the façade to set the bike to edit.*

This controller checks the inbound request to see if it contains a parameter called bikeSerialNo. If such a parameter exists, then it represents a request to edit an existing bike and as such, an implementation of RentABike will be used to fetch the appropriate bike, which will then be handed off to editBike.jsp. Conversely, if the parameter does not exist, then this request is to create a new bike, and all the fields on bikes.jsp will remain blank.

Finally, Example 2-10 gives the controller that lets you submit the new or updated bike.

**Example 2-10.** SubmitBikeController.java

```java
package com.springbook;
import org.springframework.web.servlet.mvc.Controller;
import org.springframework.web.servlet.ModelAndView;
import javax.servlet.http.HttpServletRequest;
import javax.servlet.http.HttpServletResponse;

public class SubmitBikeController implements Controller {
    private RentABike facade;

    public RentABike getFacade() { return facade; }

    public void setFacade(RentABike facade) { this.facade = facade; }

    public ModelAndView handleRequest(HttpServletRequest request,
        HttpServletResponse response) throws Exception {

        Bike bike = new Bike(request.getParameter("manufacturer"),
            request.getParameter("model"),
            Integer.parseInt(request.getParameter("frame")),
            request.getParameter("serialNo"),
            Double.parseDouble(request.getParameter("weight")),
            request.getParameter("status"));
        facade.saveBike(bike);
        return new ModelAndView("bikes.jsp", "rentaBike", facade);
    }
}
```

*Here's the code that actually saves a bike. You're going through a whole lot of effort to separate the model and view, with the hope that the code will be easier to extend and maintain later.*

This final controller takes the inbound parameters from the request to create an instance of Bike with the appropriate values and then save it to the RentABike. The user is then returned to the original bikes.jsp page, where the list of bikes will reflect the new state of the database.

## The context

Within the context, you'll wire together the model, façade, and UI. You'll want to specify the controller and view objects. You'll also need to configure a special object, called a dispatcher, within the configuration. First, you'll need to register the top-level dispatcher and your new taglibs with Tomcat in web.xml (Example 2-11).

**Example 2-11.** web.xml

```
<!DOCTYPE web-app
PUBLIC "-//Sun Microsystems, Inc.//DTD Web Application 2.2//EN"
"http://java.sun.com/j2ee/dtds/web-app_2_2.dtd">
<web-app>
<taglib>
    <taglib-uri>http://java.sun.com/jstl/core</taglib-uri>
    <taglib-location>/WEB-INF/lib/c.tld</taglib-location>
</taglib>
<servlet>
    <servlet-name>rentaBikeApp</servlet-name>
    <servlet-class>
            org.springframework.web.servlet.DispatcherServlet
    </servlet-class>
    <load-on-startup>1</load-on-startup>
</servlet>
<servlet-mapping>
    <servlet-name>rentaBikeApp</servlet-name>
    <url-pattern>*.bikes</url-pattern>
</servlet-mapping>
</web-app>
```

Notice also that you have now defined a new URL suffix (*.bikes*) for use with the application. Any URL ending with *.bikes* will be passed in to the rentaBikeApp servlet.

Next, build a Spring context in \\*war*\\*WEB-INF*\\ called rentaBikeApp-servlet.xml, which has your controllers and views in it. Later, you'll add forms and validation as well, but we'll quit here for now (Example 2-12).

**Example 2-12.** rentaBikeApp-servlet.xml

```
<beans>
    <bean id="rentaBike" class="com.springbook.ArrayListRentABike">
        <property name="storeName"><value>Bruce's Bikes</value></property>
    </bean>

    <bean id="bikesController" class="com.springbook.BikesController">
        <property name="facade"><ref bean="rentaBike"/></property>
    </bean>

    <bean id="editBikeController" class="com.springbook.EditBikeController">
        <property name="facade"><ref bean="rentaBike"/></property>
    </bean>

    <bean id="submitBikeController" class="com.springbook.SubmitBikeController">
        <property name="facade"><ref bean="rentaBike"/></property>
    </bean>
```

**Example 2-12.** rentaBikeApp-servlet.xml (continued)

```xml
<bean id="urlMapping"
    class="org.springframework.web.servlet.handler.SimpleUrlHandlerMapping">
    <property name="mappings">
        <props>
            <prop key="/bikes.bikes">bikesController</prop>
            <prop key="/editBike.bikes">editBikeController</prop>
            <prop key="/newBike.bikes">editBikeController</prop>
            <prop key="/submitBike.bikes">submitBikeController</prop>
        </props>
    </property>
</bean>
</beans>
```

Your Ant `build.xml` already has everything that you need, so you're ready to build, deploy, and run your application. Simply fire off your deploy task again.

Finally, open up your browser and navigate to the virtual directory where you set up the application (for example, *http://localhost:8080/bikes. bikes*). You'll see the main page in Figure 2-2.

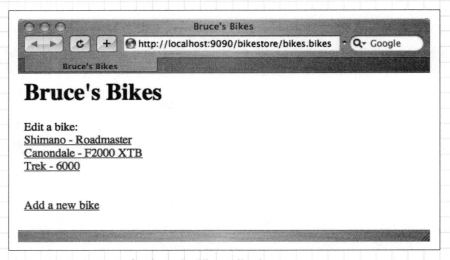

**Figure 2-2.** Main screen for the RentABike application

## What just happened?

Though the application does not look or act much differently, you've improved the structure dramatically. You've decoupled the model from the view, so that the JSP no longer knows about the underlying structure of the application. It does not need to make an explicit call to Spring to get the application context. You'll also find that it's easier to make enhancements to add form handling and validation logic. Finally, you'll see that the new structure is much easier to test. In fact, you'll be able to call the controller directly from a test case, outside of Tomcat, and verify that the structure and content of the returned model is correct.

---

### Why Web MVC?

You may ask yourself why the creators of Spring would invent an MVC framework from scratch. Shouldn't the Spring framework make it easy to use other frameworks, instead of reinventing the wheel? In fact, Rod Johnson, creator of the Spring framework, says this:

> We don't believe in reinventing wheels, except if they're not perfectly round. We didn't feel that any existing web framework was ideal, and wanted to give developers an additional choice. In particular, there were a number of issues with Struts that prompted me to design a new framework, rather than just integrate with it, such as Struts' dependence on concrete inheritance; the code duplication that typically results from enforced extension of ActionForm; and Struts 1.1's lack of interceptors as well as actions.

Clearly, Web MVC is unusual in one way: in every other case, Spring makes it easier to use an existing standard or technology, rather than inventing yet another MVC framework. Why would you employ Web MVC rather than its competitors?

- You need a framework that better supports testing. Struts is hard to test. MVC has some simple innovations that make it easier to mock. It's also easy to invoke a controller and return a model within a test case that runs outside of the servlet container.
- You place extra value on consistency. With Web MVC, you'll see consistent application of the exception model, configuration, and dependency injection.
- You have the freedom to use a less popular standard, and can tolerate the risk.

---

# Enhancing the Web Application

The code that you've seen so far begins to provide much needed organization with distinct models, views, and controllers. In this section, we'll add validation logic, a resolver, and input forms.

These enhancements will add better organization to your code and save you time and effort. Like many MVC frameworks, these classic enhancements make it easier to handle the classic flow of control that you generally get with web applications:

*Resolvers*

As your application grows, you'll want to refer to each page with a logical name rather than a full path. The resolver manages the details, like the extension and the path, letting you specify these details in your configuration.

*Form*

These input JSPs make it easy to manage user input, providing easy place holders for data, and a work flow for forms submission. Forms are separated into the view, and controller. The physical view can utilize a special Spring tag library to bind form fields to POJO properties.

*Validators*

These beans work with input forms to make it easy to handle business validation. They have no dependencies on Spring's Web MVC—you need only implement an interface—so it's easy to package your validation with your business logic.

These simple enhancements let you manage the flow of control in a manner that's consistent and organized. It also lets you keep code in a consistent place, and keep coupling to a bare minimum.

## How do I do that?

We're going to code our enhancements in two distinct steps. First, we'll configure the resolver. To do that, we're going to need to change the configuration in the rentaBikeApp-Servlet.xml by adding the following element (Example 2-13).

**Example 2-13.** rentaBikeApp-Servlet.xml

```
<bean id="viewResolver"
class="org.springframework.web.servlet.view.InternalResourceViewResolver">
   <property name="viewClass">
      <value>org.springframework.web.servlet.view.JstlView</value>
   </property>
   <property name="suffix"><value>.jsp</value></property>
</bean>
```

You can also add a prefix in addition to a suffix—for instance, if you store your JSPs in a subfolder or alternate path.

You'll also change the controller. This controller's purpose is to handle form submission. In the previous lab, this controller used the

HttpServletRequest's parameters to access the form values, but now, it will use a POJO (Example 2-14).

**Example 2-14.** SubmitBikeController.java

```java
public class SubmitBikeController extends SimpleFormController {
    private RentABike facade;

    public RentABike getFacade() { return facade; }

    public void setFacade(RentABike facade) { this.facade = facade; }

    public ModelAndView onSubmit(Object command)
            throws ServletException{

        Bike bike = (Bike)command;
        facade.saveBike(bike);
        return new ModelAndView(new RedirectView(getSuccessView()),
            "rentaBike", facade);
    }

    protected Object formBackingObject(HttpServletRequest request)
            throws Exception {

        Bike bike = new Bike();
        if(request.getParameter("bikeSerialNo") != null)
            bike = facade.getBike(request.getParameter("bikeSerialNo"));
        return bike;
    }
}
```

*This class extends SimpleFormController instead of Controller, giving us form-submission-like workflow.*

*This method will fire when the form is submitted. It will choose a path based on the success or failure of the validation.*

The controller now has an onSubmit method instead of handleRequest. onSubmit takes the POJO that holds the form field values instead of a raw HttpServletRequest. The other method, formBackingObject, allows you to initialize the POJO that will be bound to the form fields on the first request to the form.

You also need to code an input form. The form in Example 2-15 is going to make use of some new Spring-specific tags imported from the Spring *taglib*, which ships with the rest of the framework.

**Example 2-15.** editBike.jsp

```jsp
<%@ page import="com.springbook.*"%>
<%@ include file="include.jsp" %>
<%@ taglib prefix="spring" uri="/spring" %>

<html>
    <head>
        <title>
            Edit Bike
        </title>
    </head>
```

**Example 2-15.** editBike.jsp (continued)

SpringBind will bind these fields to the form. You'll see some nice behaviors, like error messages that automatically get pasted if the form fails validation.

```html
<body>
    <h1>Edit Bike</h1>
    <form method="POST">
        <spring:hasBindErrors name="bike">
            <b>Please fix all errors!</b>
        </spring:hasBindErrors>
        <table border="1" cellspacing="2" cellpadding="2">
            <tr>
                <td align="right">Manufacturer:</td>
                <td>
                    <spring:bind path="bike.manufacturer">
                    <input type="text" name="manufacturer" value="<c:out
                        value="${status.value}"/>">
                    <font color="red"><c:out
                        value="${status.errorMessage}"/></font>
                    </spring:bind>
                </td>
            </tr>
            <tr>
                <td align="right">Model:</td>
                <td>
                    <spring:bind path="bike.model">
                    <input type="text" name="model" value="<c:out
                        value="${status.value}"/>">
                    <font color="red"><c:out
                        value="${status.errorMessage}"/></font>
                    </spring:bind>
                </td>
            </tr>
            <tr>
                <td align="right">Frame:</td>
                <td>
                    <spring:bind path="bike.frame">
                    <input type="text" name="frame" value="<c:out
                        value="${status.value}"/>">
                    <font color="red"><c:out
                        value="${status.errorMessage}"/></font>
                    </spring:bind>
                </td>
            </tr>
            <tr>
                <td align="right">Serial Number:</td>
                <td>
                    <spring:bind path="bike.serialNo">
                    <input type="text" name="serialNo" value="<c:out
                        value="${status.value}"/>">
                    <font color="red"><c:out
                        value="${status.errorMessage}"/></font>
                    </spring:bind>
                </td>
            </tr>
            <tr>
```

**Example 2-15.** editBike.jsp (continued)

```
            <td align="right">Weight:</td>
            <td>
              <spring:bind path="bike.weight">
                <input type="text" name="weight" value="<c:out
                    value="${status.value}"/>">
                <font color="red"><c:out
                    value="${status.errorMessage}"/></font>
              </spring:bind>
            </td>
          </tr>
          <tr>
            <td align="right">Status:</td>
            <td>
              <spring:bind path="bike.status">
                <input type="text" name="status" value="<c:out
                    value="${status.value}"/>">
                <font color="red"><c:out
                    value="${status.errorMessage}"/></font>
              </spring:bind>
            </td>
          </tr>
        </table>
        <input type="submit" value="Submit">
      </form>
    </body>
</html>
```

See how you surround the form input fields with the `<spring:bind>` tags. This allows Spring to automap the values of the input fields to our POJO command object, and later, allows it to show error messages if the validation fails. At the top of the page, you can use the `<spring:hasBindErrors>` tag (passing in our command object) to display an error summary if there are validation errors.

You'll want Spring to validate the form, so add a specific validator (Example 2-16). You can package it with a business object. The controller will apply the correct work flow, including calling the validation.

**Example 2-16.** BikeValidator.java

```java
public class BikeValidator implements Validator {
    public boolean supports(Class aClass) {
        return aClass.equals(Bike.class);
    }

    public void validate(Object o, Errors errors) {
        Bike bike = (Bike)o;
        if(bike == null) {
            errors.rejectValue("manufacturer", "Error!",
                    null, "Value required.");
```

You'll define validators and forms in the context. These set set up with dependency injection, just like other major beans in the context.

**Example 2-16.** BikeValidator.java (continued)

```java
        } else {
            if(bike.getManufacturer( ) == null ||
                "".equals(bike.getManufacturer( )))

                errors.rejectValue("manufacturer", "Value not present.",
                        null, "Manufacturer required.");

            if(bike.getModel() == null || "".equals(bike.getModel( )))
                errors.rejectValue("model", "Value not present.", null,
                    "Model is required.");
        }

    }
}
```

Next, modify the context as in (Example 2-17); also, in the *urlMapping*, point */editBike.bikes* to *editBikeForm* instead of *editBikeController*.

**Example 2-17.** rentaBikeApp-Servlet.xml, editBike.bikes should point to editBikeForm

```xml
<bean id="bikeValidator" class="com.springbook.BikeValidator"/>
<bean id="editBikeForm" class="com.springbook.SubmitBikeController">
    <property name="sessionForm"><value>true</value></property>
    <property name="commandName"><value>bike</value></property>
    <property name="commandClass">
        <value>com.springbook.Bike</value>
    </property>
    <property name="validator"><ref bean="bikeValidator"/></property>
    <property name="formView"><value>editBike</value></property>
    <property name="successView"><value>bikes.bikes</value></property>
    <property name="facade">
        <ref bean="rentaBike"/>
    </property>
</bean>
```

Next, you'll need to add the CRUD functionality to *ArrayListRentABike* that you specified earlier in the *RentABike* interface.

**Example 2-18.** ArrayListRentABike.java

```java
package com.springbook;
import java.util.*;

public class ArrayListRentABike implements RentABike {
    private String storeName;
    final List bikes = new ArrayList();

    public void setStoreName(String name) {
        this.storeName = name;
    }
```

**Example 2-18.** ArrayListRentABike.java

```java
    public String getStoreName() {
        return storeName;
    }

    private void initBikes() {
        bikes.add(new Bike("Shimano", "Roadmaster", 20, "11111", 15, "Fair"));
        bikes.add(new Bike("Cannondale", "F2000 XTR", 18, "22222", 12,
            "Excellent"));
        bikes.add(new Bike("Trek", "6000", 19, "33333", 12.4, "Fair"));
    }

    public ArrayListRentABike() {
        initBikes();
    }

    public ArrayListRentABike(String storeName) {
        this.storeName = storeName;
        initBikes();
    }

    public String toString() { return "com.springbook.RentABike: " + storeName; }

    public List getBikes() { return bikes; }

    public Bike getBike(String serialNo) {
        Iterator iter = bikes.iterator();
        while(iter.hasNext()) {
            Bike bike = (Bike)iter.next();
            if(serialNo.equals(bike.getSerialNo())) return bike;
        }
        return null;
    }

    public void saveBike(Bike bike) {
        deleteIfContains(bike);
        bikes.add(bike);
    }
    public void deleteBike(Bike bike) {
        deleteIfContains(bike);
    }

    private void deleteIfContains(Bike bike) {
        Iterator iter = bikes.iterator();
        while(iter.hasNext()) {
            Bike comp = (Bike)iter.next();
            if(comp.getManufacturer().equals(bike.getManufacturer()) &&
                comp.getModel().equals(bike.getModel())) {
                bikes.remove(comp);
                return;
            }
        }
    }
}
```

Finally, you'll need to add the Spring taglib to the *web.xml* file so that your new JSP tags will work.

**Example 2-19.** web.xml

```
<taglib>
    <taglib-uri>/spring</taglib-uri>
    <taglib-location>/WEB-INF/lib/spring.tld</taglib-location>
</taglib>
```

Go ahead and build and deploy the changed application. Figure 2-3 shows a view of what happens when you don't enter the Manufacturer or Model for a bike.

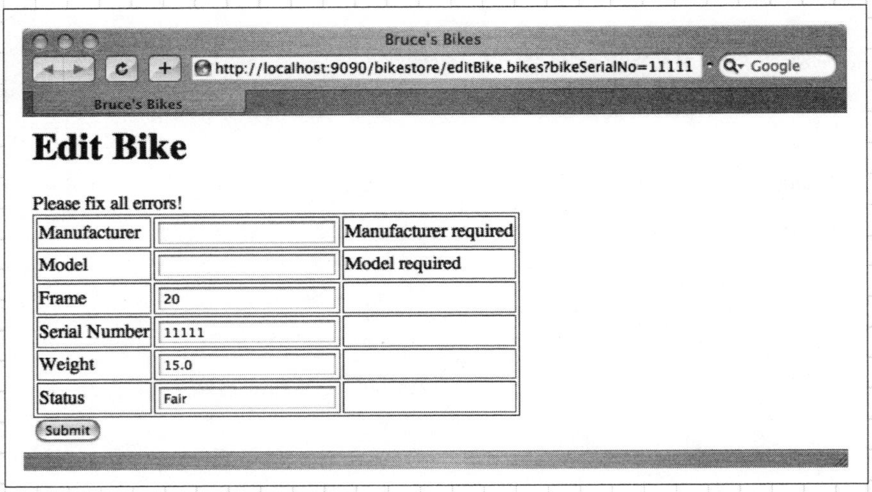

**Figure 2-3.** Manufacturer and Model missing

# What just happened?

Within the Spring configuration file, you specified the details for a view resolver. This component decouples the view from the technology that you use to render it. In this case, the resolver lets you refer to a JSP by name, instead of through a filename.

In the previous simpler example, the control was straightforward. An HTTP request triggered a controller, which then loaded another form. This application is slightly more advanced, because Spring's forms let you provide a more sophisticated workflow, and one that's more appropriate for basic input form submission and validation. In this case, you set up and configured an input form, with custom JSP tags, and then submitted it.

The Post will trigger the dispatcher, as before, and then fire the command, invoke the validator, and then return the form view if errors existed, or the success view if there were no errors. If you're familiar with the Jakarta Struts project, this flow will be familiar to you.

# Running a Test

Now that you've implemented a few simple views, it's time to do a test. We'll simply do a lightweight request, outside of the servlet container.

Part of the beauty of Web MVC is that it's much easier to test. We'll show you a couple of simple test cases that exercise the core of the user interface pretty well.

## How do I do that?

In this case, you're simply going to invoke the controller, and make sure that you get the appropriate model back. First, you can code a simple JUnit test case that invokes the BikesController (Example 2-20).

**Example 2-20.** ControllerTest.java

```
public class ControllerTest extends TestCase {

    private ApplicationContext ctx;

    public void setUp() throws Exception {
        ctx = new FileSystemXmlApplicationContext(
            "war/WEB-INF/rentaBikeApp-servlet.xml");
    }

    public void testBikesController() throws Exception {
        BikesController controller = (BikesController)
            ctx.getBean("bikesController");
        ModelAndView mav = controller.handleRequest(null, null);
        RentABike store = (RentABike) mav.getModel().get("rentaBike");
        assertNotNull(store);
        assertTrue(store.getBikes().size() == 3);
    }
}
```

*This test case loads and invokes the controller directly. No servlet container is required to build such a simple test. You can get the controller directly from the context.*

You have to load up the configuration file in order to test that Spring is loading the beans correctly. Spring provides the FileSystemXml-ApplicationContext class to load the context configuration explicitly.

Next, we'll want to test the validator to make sure it catches errors appropriately (Example 2-21).

**Example 2-21.** ControllerTest.java

```
public void testBikeValidator( ) throws Exception {
        BikeValidator v = (BikeValidator) ctx.getBean("bikeValidator");
        Bike bike = new Bike("test", "test", 1, "test", 2.00, "test");
        Errors errs = new BindException(bike, "bike");
        v.validate(bike, errs);
        assertFalse(errs.hasErrors( ));
        bike = new Bike( );
        errs = new BindException(bike, "bike");
        v.validate(bike, errs);
        assertTrue(errs.hasErrors( ));
    }
```

# What just happened?

Instead of running the test case in the container, you simply fired the controller and tested the output. Since you didn't have to test the full user interface in context, you had to do much less work to make the test case go, and you could get a basic level of testing behind you. In the next chapter, you'll see how to integrate other user interface strategies into Spring.

# Integrating Other Clients

I'd like to say that I love everything about kayaking, but that's not quite true. I hate dragging my boat to the put-in, and back out again. In fact, if I have to hike more than a couple of miles to get where I'm going, I'm probably not going to run the river. It's not that I hate hiking, or even backpacking. It's just that those in my sport don't hike with our boats enough, so we haven't usually thought through the problem.

In truth, there are a whole lot of tools that make it easier to get to the river, and most of them borrow from other sports. Backpackers routinely carry more than a hundred pounds over long distances, and a backpack harness developed by the national park system lets rangers negotiate portages and trails easily. Since many rivers travel along side railroads, it's possible to slide a kayak along them, if you've got the right harness. Certain river shoes are starting to mimic hiking boots, in terms of tread and support. To make the put-in experience more enjoyable, I need to borrow techniques and tools from other places. Or, I can just do rivers with easier access.

Other user interface frameworks do things that Spring can't. Struts has a huge community with many books and libraries; JavaServer Faces and Tapestry both add a rich component model, and Tapestry also supports complete separation of the HTML from the components. The Spring founders understand that Spring's Web MVC is not the only way to get your boat to the river. Keith Donald's Spring rich client project brings more sophisticated Swing user interfaces to Spring. Others have integrated struts, Web Work, and even tapestry with Spring. Noted consultant/authors like Rick Hightower use the emerging JavaServer Faces standard with Spring in projects. In this chapter, you'll meet David Geary, a member of the JSF Expert Group, who will walk you through a

JavaServer Faces example. In Chapter 9, you'll see some *sandbox* code
that builds a rich client.

# Building a Struts User Interface

In the first example, you'll build a portion of our user interface with
Java's most popular user interface framework, Struts. You'll also learn
how to wire it to Spring.

If you're starting a new project, you may decide to choose an alternative
to Struts. We believe that emerging MVC frameworks improve the user
and developer experience, but Struts is still the most popular choice.

## How do I do that?

The Struts user interface looks much like the web MVC interface. You'll
configure a central dispatcher. The dispatcher will send requests to a
controller, and the controller will invoke business logic in the form of
actions.

First, you need to configure Struts. That happens in two places: web.xml
configures your central dispatcher and struts-config.xml manages the
Struts Controller. Example 3-1 shows web.xml.

**Example 3-1.** web.xml

```
<!DOCTYPE web-app
    PUBLIC  "-//Sun Microsystems, Inc.//DTD Web Application 2.2//EN"
    "http://java.sun.com/j2ee/dtds/web-app_2_2.dtd">

<web-app>

    <display-name>RentABike</display-name>
    <description>
        Renting bikes for fun and profit.
    </description>

    <context-param>
        <param-name>contextConfigLocation</param-name>
        <param-value>
          /WEB-INF/rentABikeApp-servlet.xml
        </param-value>
    </context-param>

    <servlet>
      <servlet-name>SpringContext</servlet-name>
      <servlet-class>
          org.springframework.web.context.ContextLoaderServlet
```

**Example 3-1.** web.xml (continued)

```
      </servlet-class>
      <load-on-startup>1</load-on-startup>
   </servlet>

   <servlet>
      <servlet-name>RentABike</servlet-name>
      <servlet-class>
          org.apache.struts.action.ActionServlet
      </servlet-class>
      <init-param>
         <param-name>config</param-name>
         <param-value>/WEB-INF/struts-config.xml</param-value>
      </init-param>
      <init-param>
         <param-name>validate</param-name>
         <param-value>true</param-value>12
      </init-param>
      <load-on-startup>2</load-on-startup>
   </servlet>

   <servlet-mapping>
      <servlet-name>RentABike</servlet-name>
      <url-pattern>*.do</url-pattern>
   </servlet-mapping>

   <welcome-file-list>
      <welcome-file>
          start.html
      </welcome-file>
   </welcome-file-list>

   <context-param>
      <param-name>log4jConfigLocation</param-name>
      <param-value>/WEB-INF/log4j.properties</param-value>
   </context-param>

<listener>
      <listener-class>
          org.springframework.web.util.Log4jConfigListener
      </listener-class>
</listener>

<taglib>
      <taglib-uri>/spring</taglib-uri>
      <taglib-location>/WEB-INF/spring.tld</taglib-location>
</taglib>

<taglib>
      <taglib-uri>http://java.sun.com/jstl/core</taglib-uri>
      <taglib-location>/WEB-INF/c.tld</taglib-location>
</taglib>
```

*This is the main Struts servlet, called an action servlet. It will serve as the controller for the RentABike application.*

**Example 3-1.** web.xml (continued)

```
<taglib>
    <taglib-uri>/struts</taglib-uri>
    <taglib-location>/WEB-INF/struts-bean.tld</taglib-location>
</taglib>

<listener>
    <listener-class>
        org.springframework.web.context.ContextLoaderListener
    </listener-class>
</listener>
```

```
</web-app>
```

If you've seen Struts before, you understand that there's nothing new here. We configured two servlets, one for loading the Spring context and one for controlling Struts. Each is labeled in load in a particular order (Spring first, then Struts) using the `<load-on-startup>` element. We load Spring first because the Struts actions rely on the Spring-created `RentABike` object, which has to be accessible by the time Struts starts loading its own objects. Notice also that the file loads several tag libraries for use by the *.jsp* pages via the `<taglib>` element. Finally, in classic Struts style, we created a custom suffix mapping to map inbound URL requests to the Struts controller. The `<servlet-mapping>` element says that any URL request whose filename ends in ".do" will be mapped to the Struts controller. There are many books on the inner workings of Struts, and we'll not repeat them here.

Next, you'll need to configure the mappings that tie a request to individual actions (Example 3-2). This action map defines the basic flow of the application, and is part of `struts-config.xml`.

**Example 3-2.** struts-config.xml

```
<?xml version="1.0" encoding="UTF-8"?>
<!DOCTYPE struts-config PUBLIC
 "-//Apache Software Foundation//DTD Struts Configuration 1.1//EN"
 "http://jakarta.apache.org/struts/dtds/struts-config_1_1.dtd">

<struts-config>

    <form-beans>
        <form-bean name="EditBikeForm"
                    type="com.springbook.forms.EditBikeForm"/>
    </form-beans>

    <action-mappings>
```

**Chapter 3: Integrating Other Clients**

**Example 3-2.** struts-config.xml (continued)

```xml
        <action  path="/bikes"
                type="org.apache.struts.actions.ForwardAction"
                parameter="/bikes.jsp"/>

        <action  path="/editBike"
                type="org.apache.struts.actions.ForwardAction"
                parameter="/editBike.jsp"/>

        <action  path="/submitBike"
                type="com.springbook.actions.SubmitBikeAction"
                name="EditBikeForm"
                scope="request"
                validate="true"
                input="/editBike.jsp">

                <display-name>Submit Bike</display-name>

                <forward name="success" path="/bikes.jsp"/>
                <forward name="failure" path="/editBike.jsp"/>

        </action>

    </action-mappings>

</struts-config>
```

*Each entry maps a Struts action onto a jsp. When the action occurs, the request will open the new jsp. It's the road map for a Struts application.*

This file also contains definitions for any beans used to hold form information. In this case, there is a bean to hold information about the bike being edited, `EditBikeForm`.

You'll need to define a stub for the scheduling part of the application. Once again, you'll read the stub from an array list (Example 3-3).

**Example 3-3.** ArrayListRentABike.java

```java
public class ArrayListRentABike implements RentABike {
    private String storeName;
    final List bikes = new ArrayList();

    public void saveBike(Bike bike) {
        if(bikes.contains(bike)) bikes.remove(bike);
        bikes.add(bike);
    }

    public void deleteBike(Bike bike) {
        bikes.remove(bike);
    }

    public ArrayListRentABike() {
        initBikes();
    }
```

**Example 3-3.** ArrayListRentABike.java (continued)

```java
    public ArrayListRentABike (String storeName) {
        this.storeName = storeName;
        initBikes();
    }

    private void initBikes() {
        bikes.add(new Bike(1, "Shimano",
            "Roadmaster", 20, "11111", 15, "Fair"));
        bikes.add(new Bike(2, "Cannondale",
            "F2000 XTR", 18, "22222",12, "Excellent"));
        bikes.add(new Bike(3, "Trek",
            "6000", 19, "33333", 12.4, "Fair"));
    }

    public String toString() {
        return "com.springbook.ArrayListRentABike: " + storeName;
    }

    public String getStoreName() {
        return storeName;
    }

    public void setStoreName(String storeName) {
        this.storeName = storeName;
    }

    public List getBikes() {
        return bikes;
    }

    public Bike getBike(String serialNo) {
        Iterator iter = bikes.iterator();
        while(iter.hasNext()) {
            Bike bike = (Bike)iter.next();
            if(serialNo.equals(bike.getSerialNo())) return bike;
        }
        return null;
    }

    public Bike getBike(int bikeId) {
        if(bikeId > bikes.size()) return null;
        return (Bike)bikes.get(bikeId);
    }

    //etc...
}
```

Each action will need access to your façade. You'll build a base action (Example 3-4), which gets the bike shop façade from the Spring context.

---

**Chapter 3: Integrating Other Clients**

**Example 3-4.** BaseAction.java

```java
public abstract class BaseAction extends Action {

    private RentABike rentABike;

    public void setServlet(ActionServlet actionServlet) {
        super.setServlet(actionServlet);
        ServletContext servletContext = actionServlet.getServletContext();
        WebApplicationContext wac =
            WebApplicationContextUtils.
                getRequiredWebApplicationContext(servletContext);
        this.rentABike = (RentABike) wac.getBean("RentABike");
    }

    protected RentABIke getRentABike() {
        return rentABike;
    }

    // Plus other utility methods suitable for a base action

}
```

*Get the context and set the rentABike instance variable, so that the Struts actions can access the façade.*

Remember that you have to define the RentABike bean in rentABikeApp-servlet.xml (Example 3-5).

**Example 3-5.** rentaBike-Servlet.xml

```xml
<beans>
    <bean id="rentaBike" class="com.springbook.ArrayListRentABike">
        <property name="storeName"><value>Bruce's Bikes</value></property>
    </bean>

    <!-- etc. -->
</beans>
```

Each action then does its job (Example 3-6).

**Example 3-6.** SubmitBikeAction.java

```java
public class SubmitBikeAction extends BaseAction {

    public SubmitBikeAction() {
        super();
    }

    public ActionForward execute(
        ActionMapping mapping,
        ActionForm form,
        HttpServletRequest request,
        HttpServletResponse response)
        throws java.lang.Exception {

        EditBikeForm editBikeForm = (EditBikeForm) form;
```

This code uses the form submission flow. You configured the form in struts-config.xml, and you'll define it below.

**Example 3-6.** SubmitBikeAction.java (continued)

```java
        Bike bike = new Bike();
        bike.setManufacturer(editBikeForm.getManufacturer());
        bike.setModel(editBikeForm.getModel());
        bike.setFrame(editBikeForm.getFrame());
        bike.setSerialNo(editBikeForm.getSerialNo());
        bike.setWeight(editBikeForm.getWeight());

        try {
            this.rentABike.saveBike(bike);
            return mapping.findForward("success");
        } catch (Exception ex) {
            return mapping.findForward("failure");
        }

    }
}
```

You'll need to use Struts tags to render the pages. Example 3-7 is the *EditBike.jsp* page.

**Example 3-7.** EditBike.jsp

```jsp
<%@ page import="com.springbook.*"%>
<%@ include file="include.jsp" %>
<%@ taglib prefix="spring" uri="/spring" %>
<%@ taglib uri="/WEB-INF/struts-html-el.tld" prefix="html-el" %>

<html>
    <head>
        <title>
            Edit Bike
        </title>
    </head>
    <body>
        <h1>Edit Bike</h1>
        <form method="POST">
            <table border="1" cellspacing="2" cellpadding="2">
                <tr>
                    <td align="right">Manufacturer:</td>
                    <td>
                        <html-el:text property="manufacturer" size="25"
                        maxlength="50" styleClass="textBox" tabindex="1" />
                    </td>
                </tr>
                <tr>
                    <td align="right">Model:</td>
                    <td>
                        <html-el:text property="model" size="25"
                        maxlength="50" styleClass="textBox" tabindex="1" />
                    </td>
                </tr>
```

Example 3-7. EditBike.jsp (continued)

```
            <tr>
                <td align="right">Frame:</td>
                <td>
                    <html-el:text property="frame" size="25"
                    maxlength="50" styleClass="textBox" tabindex="1" />
                </td>
            </tr>
            <tr>
                <td align="right">Serial Number:</td>
                <td>
                    <html-el:text property="serialNo" size="25"
                    maxlength="50" styleClass="textBox" tabindex="1" />
                </td>
            </tr>
            <tr>
                <td align="right">Weight:</td>
                <td>
                    <html-el:text property="weight" size="25"
                    maxlength="50" styleClass="textBox" tabindex="1" />
                </td>
            </tr>
            <tr>
                <td align="right">Status:</td>
                <td>
                    <html-el:text property="status" size="25"
                    maxlength="50" styleClass="textBox" tabindex="1" />
                </td>
            </tr>
        </table>
        <html-el:submit styleClass="normal">
            Submit Bike
        </html-el:submit>
    </form>
  </body>
</html>
```

There's nothing special here. You're using standard Struts tags. Finally, you'll need to code up the EditBikeForm to transfer HTML element values to the Controller (Example 3-8).

**Example 3-8.** EditBikeForm.java

```
public class EditBikeForm extends ActionForm {

    private String manufacturer;
    private String model;
    private int frame;
    private String serialNo;
    private double weight;
    private String status;
```

**Example 3-8.** EditBikeForm.java (continued)

```java
public void reset(ActionMapping mapping, HttpServletRequest request) {
    manufacturer = null;
    model = null;
    frame = 0;
    serialNo = null;
    weight = 0.0;
    status = null;
}

public ActionErrors validate(
    ActionMapping mapping,
    HttpServletRequest request) {
    ActionErrors errors = new ActionErrors();

    String mappingName = mapping.getPath();

    if (mappingName.equalsIgnoreCase("/SubmitBike")) {
        if (manufacturer == null
            || manufacturer.trim().length() == 0) {
            errors.add(
                "bike",
                new ActionError("error.manufacturer.required));
        }

        if (model == null
            || model.trim().length() == 0) {
            errors.add(
                "bike",
                new ActionError("error.mo del.required"));
        }
    }

    return errors;
}

public EditBikeForm() {
    super();
}

public void setManufacturer(String manufacturer) {
    this.manufacturer = manufacturer;
}

public String getManufacturer() {
    return manufacturer;
}

public void setModel(String model) {
    this.model = model;
}
```

*This method handles the Struts validation workflow. It sets form data in the incoming request parameter. It returns any errors when it's done.*

**Example 3-8.** EditBikeForm.java (continued)

```java
    public String getModel( ) {
        return model;
    }

    public void setFrame(int frame) {
        this.frame = frame;
    }

    public int getFrame( ) {
        return frame;
    }

    public void setSerialNo(String serialNo) {
        this.serialNo = serialNo;
    }

    public String setSerialNo( ) {
        return serialNo;
    }

    public void setWeight(Double weight) {
        this.weight = weight;
    }

    public Double getWeight( ) {
        return weight;
    }

    public void setStatus(String status) {
        this.status = status;
    }

    public String getStatus( ) {
        return status;
    }

}
```

And you can run the application.

As before, you'll want to test what you have written (Example 3-9). One thing that is often important to test in applications like this are the validation rules for the forms being submitted. You can easily test just the validation rules with a simple JUnit test.

**Example 3-9.** StrutsTest.java

```java
public void testBikeValidation( ) throws Exception {
    ActionMapping mapping = new ActionMapping( );
    mapping.setPath("/SubmitBike");
    EditBikeForm ebf = new EditBikeForm( );
```

Example 3-9. StrutsTest.java (continued)

```
    ebf.setManufacturer("a manufacturer");
    ebf.setModel("a model");
    ActionErrors errors = ebf.validate(mapping, null);
    assertEquals(0, errors.size( ));
    ebf = new EditBikeForm( );
    ebf.setManufacturer("a manufacturer");
    ebf.setModel("");
    errors = ebf.validate(mapping, null);
    assertEquals(1, errors.size( ));
}
```

For more complex testing of the workings of the Actions and ActionMappings themselves, we recommend starting with Lu Jian's fine article "Unit Test Your Struts Application" at *http://www.onjava.com/pub/a/onjava/2004/09/22/test-struts.html*.

## What just happened?

Not much. You see a typical Struts application, without Spring. Figure 3-1 shows the flow of control. A client issues an HTTP request. The request goes through a central dispatcher. You configured the central dispatcher in web.xml. A Struts mapping (in struts-config.xml) associates a request with a controller, and the dispatcher routes control to the appropriate controller, which inherits from servlet. Struts then can invoke business logic through actions. Struts, like Spring, also has a generic form submission workflow that manages validation, and error form processing. The key question is this: how does RentABike get access to the Spring context?

As you've seen, the pieces of your Spring application will normally resolve dependencies through the container. Spring instantiates the objects in the application and injects dependencies in the form of properties, into the application. When you're integrating third-party frameworks, dependency injection is not always possible.

This version of the application manages the flow through Struts. When Struts gets a request, it reads the mapping file, which associates an HTTP request with a controller. The controller fires an action. This Struts action then fires a method.

The Struts action is where Spring comes in. Each action inherits from a base action. This base action gets the Spring context from the servlet context. Then, the application easily retrieves our façade, and has access to all of the business methods in the application.

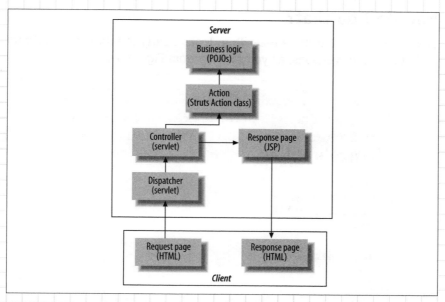

**Figure 3-1.** Struts applications have a central dispatcher, a servlet controller, actions, and JSP response pages

# Using JSF with Spring

In this section you'll see how to use JavaServer Faces and Spring together. Then we'll see how you can use the JSF expression language to access Spring beans.

JSF, like Spring MVC and Tapestry, is a second-generation web application framework. The first generation, represented by frameworks such as Struts, have taught us a lot over the past three or four years, and better frameworks have evolved as a result. For example, both JSF and Tapestry have component models, which makes it easier to extend those frameworks and share that work with others.

JSF, Tapestry, and Spring MVC also support *value bindings*—wiring HTML elements (in the case of Spring MVC) or components (JSF and Tapestry) to JavaBean properties. In that simple mechanism lies a lot of power. More about that later…

In the first example, you will implement Bruce's Bike Shop using JSF and Spring.

## How do I do that?

The JSF version of Bruce's Bike Store looks nearly identical to the Struts and Spring MVC versions, as you can see from Figure 3-2.

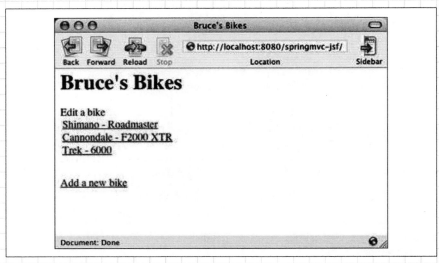

**Figure 3-2.** JSF version of the main page

You can dive right into the JSF version of *bikes.jsp*:

```
<%@ taglib prefix="f" uri="http://java.sun.com/jsf/core" %>
<%@ taglib prefix="h" uri="http://java.sun.com/jsf/html" %>

<html>
  <f:view>
    <head>
      <title>
        <h:outputText value="#{rentABike.storeName}"/>
      </title>
    </head>

    <body>
      <h1><h:outputText value="#{rentABike.storeName}"/></h1>

      <h:outputText value="Edit a bike"/>

      <h:form>
        <h:dataTable value="#{rentABike.bikes}" var="bike">
          <h:column>
            <h:commandLink action="#{editBikeController.editBike}">
              <h:outputText
          value="#{bike.manufacturer} - #{bike.model}"/>
```

*These tags are from the JSF tag libraries.*

```
                   <f:param name="bikeSerialNo" value="#{bike.serialNo}"/>
                </h:commandLink>
            </h:column>
        </h:dataTable>

        <h:outputText value="<br/><br/>" escape="false"/>

        <h:commandLink action="#{editBikeController.newBike}">
            <h:outputText value="Add a new bike"/>
        </h:commandLink>
      </h:form>
    </body>
  </f:view>
</html>
```

The preceding code uses JSF tags, such as f:view, h:form, h:outputText, and h:dataTable to create the same web page that you implemented with Spring MVC and Struts. You start by importing the JSF tag libraries with the taglib directive.

As you use the JSF tags, keep in mind that tag names represent component/renderer pairs. Components maintain state and renderers generate markup. For example, the h:dataTable tag represents the data component paired with the table renderer. This distinguishes JSF from component-less frameworks such as Struts, whose JSP tags typically generate markup directly.

The first thing to do in this JSP page is create a view. All JSP pages in a JSF application must enclose all component tags, such as h:outputText and h:commandLink, in a view component. That component is represented by the f:view tag.

After the f:view tag, you use an h:outputText tag to set the window title to a value binding—#{rentABike.storeName}—which references the bike store's name. Notice you're using value bindings such as #{bike.model} and #{bike.serialNo} throughout the rest of the page to access the bikes in the bike store.

A few things about this JSP page are worth mentioning before moving on:

1. h:dataTable iterates over an array of bikes and makes each bike available as a variable named bike. Notice the similarity to JSTL tags, many of which also have var attributes.

2. Besides value bindings that represent JavaBean *properties*, such as #{rentABike.storeName}, you are also using value bindings that bind to *methods*; for example, the action attribute of the link that creates a new bike—#{editBikeController.newBike}—represents the newBike

method of the editBikeController. Using Java reflection, JSF will invoke that method when you activate the link.

3. You're using the f:param tag to attach a parameter to the request when that tag's enclosing h:commandLink is activated. That request parameter's name is bikeSerialNo; its value is #{bike.serialNo}, which represents the serial number of the current bike. You will use that request parameter in the editBikeController.editBike( ) method. That method is specified with the action attribute for the first h:commandLink tag in the preceeding JSP page.

Now you need to implement the editBike.jsp, as shown in Figure 3-3.

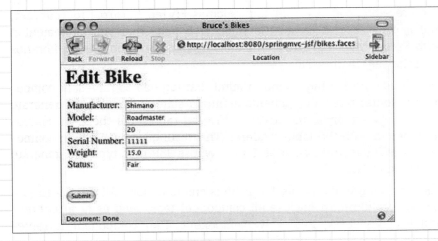

**Figure 3-3.** JSF version of the editBike.jsp

Here's how you implement editBike.jsp with JSF:

```
<%@ taglib prefix="f" uri="http://java.sun.com/jsf/core" %>
<%@ taglib prefix="h" uri="http://java.sun.com/jsf/html" %>

<html>
    <f:view>
        <head>
            <title>
                <h:outputText value="#{rentABike.storeName}"/>
            </title>
        </head>

        <body>
            <h1><h:outputText value="Edit Bike"/></h1>

            <h:form>
                <h:panelGrid columns="2">
```

```
                <h:outputText value="Manufacturer:"/>
                <h:panelGroup>
                    <h:inputText id="manufacturer" required="true"
                        value="#{editBikeController.bikeToEdit.manufacturer}"/>
                    <h:message for="manufacturer" style="color: Red"/>
                </h:panelGroup>
                <h:outputText value="Model:"/>
                <h:panelGroup>
                    <h:inputText id="model" required="true"
                            value="#{editBikeController.bikeToEdit.model}"/>
                    <h:message for="model" style="color: Red"/>
                </h:panelGroup>

                <h:outputText value="Frame:"/>
                <h:panelGroup>
                    <h:inputText id="frame" required="true"
                            value="#{editBikeController.bikeToEdit.frame}"
                        converter="javax.faces.Integer"/>
                    <h:message for="frame" style="color: Red"/>
                </h:panelGroup>

                <h:outputText value="Serial Number:"/>
                <h:panelGroup>
                    <h:inputText id="serialNo" required="true"
                            value="#{editBikeController.bikeToEdit.serialNo}"/>
                    <h:message for="serialNo" style="color: Red"/>
                </h:panelGroup>

                <h:outputText value="Weight:"/>
                <h:panelGroup>
                    <h:inputText id="weight" required="true"
                            value="#{editBikeController.bikeToEdit.weight}"
                        converter="javax.faces.Double"/>
                    <h:message for="weight" style="color: Red"/>
                </h:panelGroup>

                <h:outputText value="Status:"/>
                <h:panelGroup>
                    <h:inputText id="status" required="true"
                            value="#{editBikeController.bikeToEdit.status}"/>
                    <h:message for="status" style="color: Red"/>
                </h:panelGroup>
            </h:panelGrid>

            <h:outputText value="<br/><br/>" escape="false"/>

            <h:commandButton value="Submit"
            action="#{editBikeController.saveBike}"/>
        </h:form>
    </body>
  </f:view>
</html>
```

This grouping defines the grouping for the manufacturer control. If the user value doesn't pass validation, you'll get an error message in red.

Once again, you're using JSF tags to create a web page. You use converters to convert each bike's frame and weight properties from strings to integers and floats, respectively. You're also performing server-side validation by specifying required field values. Finally, you use h:message tags to display error messages next to offending text fields, in red, when the user neglects to enter a value for a required field, as shown in Figure 3-4.

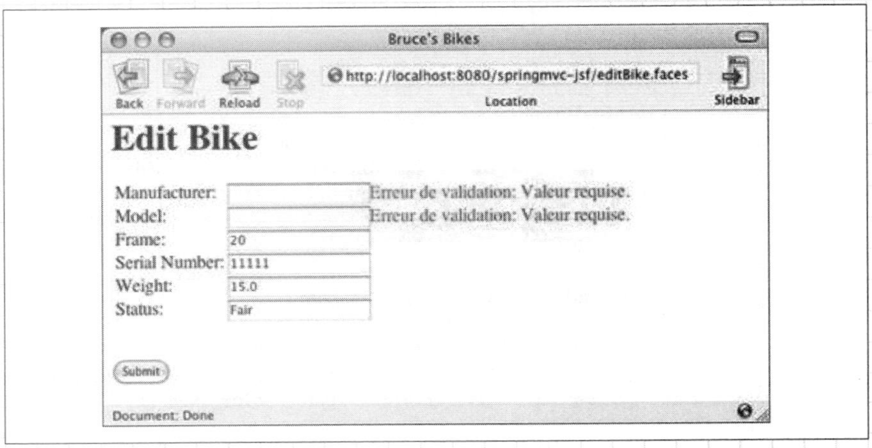

**Figure 3-4.** JSF error messages in French because the browser is set to prefer French

Notice the error messages in the preceding snapshot are in French. That's because the user has set his browser settings to prefer French. JSF detects that browser setting and automatically localizes error messages.

Now that you've implemented the requisite JSP pages for Bruce's Bike Shop, it's time to specify navigation between those pages. In the faces configuration file, you enter the following:

```xml
<?xml version="1.0"?>

<!DOCTYPE faces-config PUBLIC
    "-//Sun Microsystems, Inc.//DTD JavaServer Faces Config 1.0//EN"
    "http://java.sun.com/dtd/web-facesconfig_1_0.dtd">

<faces-config>
    <navigation-rule>
        <navigation-case>
            <from-outcome>edit</from-outcome>
            <to-view-id>/editBike.jsp</to-view-id>
        </navigation-case>
    </navigation-rule>
</faces-config>
```

*The jsf-config file looks a lot like the Struts config file. You specify an action and a result, in the form of a JSP page.*

```
<navigation-rule>
    <navigation-case>
        <from-outcome>bikes</from-outcome>
        <to-view-id>/bikes.jsp</to-view-id>
    </navigation-case>
</navigation-rule>
</faces-config>
```

Navigation rules are easy to define and read. Here, you've defined one rule that loads /editBike.jsp whenever an action returns an outcome of "edit" and a second rule that loads /bikes.jsp whenever an action returns an outcome of "bikes". Those outcomes are returned by the following EditBikeController methods:

```
public class EditBikeController {
    ...
    public String editBike() {
        HttpServletRequest request = (HttpServletRequest)
                                     FacesContext.getCurrentInstance().
                                     getExternalContext().getRequest();
        bikeToEdit = facade.getBike(request.getParameter("bikeSerialNo"));
        return "edit";
    }

    public String newBike() {
        bikeToEdit = new Bike();
        return "edit";
    }

    public String saveBike() {
        facade.saveBike(bikeToEdit);
        return "bikes";
    }
}
```

The preceding methods are invoked by JSF. You ensure that invocation by specifying those methods as actions for the links in /bikes.jsp and the submit button in /editBike.jsp.

## What just happened?

You just implemented a JSF application that:

- Converts and validates user input
- Navigates from one JSP page to another
- Automatically transports data from web forms to bean properties and vice versa

Notice the last bullet item listed above. Previously, I mentioned that value bindings were a powerful concept. To grasp just how powerful value bindings are, it pays to consider the most fundamental aspect of any web application: binding fields in a form to model objects.

With Struts, you accomplish that task by manually transferring data from a form bean and pushing it to your model. That involves a fair bit of overhead: implementing an action class, mapping that action class to a URL in the Struts configuration file, invoking form bean methods to extract field values, invoking model object methods to set the corresponding bean properties, and, if you are a consientious developer, implementing a test class that tests your action. Wow. That's a lot of work.

With second-generation web application frameworks like JSF, Tapestry, and Spring MVC, however, you simply use a value binding. In JSF, you specify a value binding in a JSP page. For example:

```
<h:inputText value="#{someBean.someProperty}"/>
```

Then you just implement the method:

```
public class SomeBean {
    ...
    public int setSomeProperty(int property) { ... }
}
```

That's all there is to it. No action class, no action mapping, no manually transferring form bean properties to model properties. Value bindings remove all that overhead. Also, notice that value bindings are not invasive: the SomeBean need not know that it's a backing bean for a JSP page in a JSF application because there are no ties to the JSF API. That makes JSF backing beans easy to test.

# Integrating JSF with Spring

Spring comes with a JSF variable resolver that lets you use JSF and Spring together. You can access Spring beans using JSF and vice versa. Integrating JSF and Spring lets you tap into the capabilities of two of the most powerful server-side Java frameworks.

## How do I do that?

You already did! In the previous example you used value bindings to bind JSF components to model objects. For example, in /bike.jsp, you did this:

```
...
<h:form>
    <h:dataTable value="#{rentABike.bikes}" var="bike">
```

```
                <h:column>
                   ...
                </h:column>
             </h:dataTable>
          ...
       </h:form>
       ...
```

The #{rentABike.bikes} value binding references the bikes property of
the bean named rentABike. Recall that previously, the rentABike bean
was defined in a Spring configuration file, like this:

```
<?xml version="1.0" encoding="UTF-8"?>
<!DOCTYPE beans PUBLIC "-//SPRING//DTD BEAN//EN" "http://www.
springframework.org/dt\
d/spring-beans.dtd">

<beans>
    <bean name="rentABike" class="com.springbook.ArrayListRentABike">
        <property name="storeName"><value>Bruce's Bikes</value></property>
    </bean>

    ...
</beans>
```

Things are no different in the JSF version of Bruce's Bike Shop, which
means that *the JSF expression #{rentABike.bikes} accesses a Spring
bean.* That's made possible by the DelegatingVariableResolver from the
org.springframework.web.jsf package. You declare that variable
resolver, which extends the JSF expression language to include references to Spring beans, in the faces configuration file:

```
<faces-config>
    <application>
        <variable-resolver>
            org.springframework.web.jsf.DelegatingVariableResolver
        </variable-resolver>
    </application>
    ...
</faces-config>
```

# What just happened?

You saw how easy it is to integrate JSF and Spring. You can access
Spring beans with the JSF expression language. That seamless integration makes it easy to use these two powerful frameworks together.

## What about...

...JSF managed beans? Like Spring, JSF has a bean factory. You specify managed beans in a faces configuration file and JSF instantiates and initializes those beans. In our JSF version of Bruce's Bike Shop, we didn't use any managed beans; instead, we used Spring beans exclusively. However, most web applications built on JSF and Spring will have ample quantities of both Spring beans and managed beans.

# Using JDBC

On my first trip down the Cossatot River, the first two sections were easy and beautiful, but I couldn't enjoy them fully. I'd never really been on a class IV rapid, and I'd read that section three would start out with vengeance: five waterfalls ranging from six to ten feet, with the coup de grace being the fourth drop, called Washing Machine. I unintentionally ran two of the five backwards. But every advanced paddler needs to start somewhere, and I became addicted.

To this point, you've seen some real user interface work, but you haven't attached our application to anything with real meat. Like the Five Falls section on the Cossatot, this is where traditional development gets especially treacherous. In this section, we'll address perhaps the core concern of most enterprise applications: persistence. In this chapter, you'll focus on adding persistence with Spring's JDBC helper-classes. In the next, you'll extend that solution to work with full object relational mapping frameworks. In either case, you'll find that Spring provides tremendous value.

## Setting Up the Database and Schema

If you don't already have a relational database, it's time to set one up, define the schema for our application, and tweak our Ant build appropriately. Don't worry. It will go quickly. We'll use MySQL. You can then define some scripts that build the schema, and an Ant task to create the database from a script.

I'm directionally challenged, but kayakers have a tremendous advantage that most hikers don't share. Hikers can get easily lost as they take on more advanced hikes. My rivers don't move. They stay in the river beds, and flow one direction. I never have to worry about getting lost, as long as I can find the put-in and the take-out. Spring is like the river that lends structure and direction to your journey. It doesn't provide the database or transactions or remoting, but makes those services more consistent and easier to use.

## How do I do that?

First, you'll get and install MySQL. You can find it at *http://mysql.org*. Download it and follow the installation directions. Make sure to pay special attention to the instructions for initializing and modifying the user accounts for the installation; the instructions can vary greatly from one version to the next.

Start the MySQL daemon and make sure things are working by creating a database, as in Example 4-1.

**Example 4-1.** Using mysql client to list databases

```
mysql> create database bikestore;
Query OK, 1 row affected (0.00 sec)

mysql> show databases;
+------------+
| Database   |
+------------+
| bikestore  |
| mysql      |
| test       |
+------------+
3 rows in set (0.00 sec)
```

Your application is going to talk to MySQL through a JDBC driver. You've got to tell the JVM how to find it. You'll want to download the latest release version of the *Mysql Connector/J* library and make it available to your project's classpath. In this case, we've copied it into the */lib* folder underneath the main project folder.

Next, you can create the database schema. You could issue commands directly against the database. You'd be able to quickly establish a few tables, and you'd get immediate feedback if you made any syntax errors. But there are also a few downsides to that approach:

- You wouldn't be able to automate the process. If you wanted to create the database on another machine, you couldn't.

- You wouldn't have the DDL (data definition language). The DDL can also help you communicate with others that may want to read your code, or help them set up the environment to test the code.
- Later, when you use an object relational mapper, it's safer to use a script than to point it directly to the database.

Instead, you'll create a file with your database schema and data, and store it in the project's /db folder, which you created earlier. For each table, you'll use an identifier, which makes it easier to build consistent code, and a simple schema, which handles the identifiers consistently. You'll also see a database table column for each major field. For the most part, your design will let you have one class per table, but not exclusively. Some of the relationships will require extra relationship tables (Example 4-2).

**Example 4-2.** rentabike.sql

```sql
drop database bikestore;

create database bikestore;

use bikestore;

create table bikes (
    bikeId int(11) not null auto_increment,
    manufacturer char(50) not null,
    model char(50) not null,
    frame int(11) not null default '0',
    serialNo char(20) not null,
    weight double not null default '0',
    `status` char(15) not null,
    primary key (bikeId));

create table customers (
    custId int(11) not null auto_increment,
    firstname char(50) not null,
    lastname char(50) not null,
    primary key (custId));

create table reservations (
    resId int(11) not null auto_increment,
    bikeId int(11) not null,
    custId int(11) not null,
    resDate date not null,
    primary key (resId));
```

*This statement is shorthand for deleting all of the tables in the database. Use this script with caution! You wouldn't ever want to point your database configuration files at the production database.*

After creating the tables, you should assign all permissions to your account so that your code can access the data.

You should try to verify your driver with the simple test shown in Example 4-3, which opens the driver.

**Example 4-3.** ControllerTest.java

```java
public void testJDBC( ) throws Exception {
    try {
        System.setProperty("jdbc.drivers", "com.mysql.jdbc.Driver");
        Connection conn =
DriverManager.getConnection("jdbc:mysql://localhost/bikestore");
    } catch (Exception ex) {
        fail("Failed to open connection:" + ex.getMessage( ));
    }
    assertTrue(true);
}
```

Example 4-4 creates some sample data. This approach is nice, because once you start testing, it allows you to start with a consistent set of test data for each test case.

**Example 4-4.** rentabike.sql

```sql
insert into bikes values(1, "Shimano", "Roadmaster", 20, "11111", 15, "Fair");
insert into bikes values(2, "Cannondale", "F2000 XTR", 18, "22222",12, "Excellent");
insert into bikes values(3, "Trek","6000", 19, "33333", 12.4, "Fair");

insert into customers values(1, "Justin", "Gehtland");
insert into customers values(2, "Bruce", "Tate");

insert into reservations values(1, 2, 2, '2004-09-15');
insert into reservations values(2, 3, 1, '2004-10-07');
```

Finally, you'll modify your Ant build script to use the *rentabike.sql* file to create your database. To do so, you'll have to provide a couple of new properties, as well as a classpath that points to the MySQL driver in your */lib* folder.

**Example 4-5.** build.xml

```xml
<property name="database.url" value="jdbc:mysql://localhost/bikestore"/>
<property name="database.username" value="bikestore"/>

<path id="mysql.class.path">
    <pathelement location="${war.dir}/WEB-INF/lib/
        mysql-connector-java-3.0.14-production-bin.jar"/>
</path>

<target name="create.tables">
    <sql driver="com.mysql.jdbc.Driver"
        url="${database.url}"
        userid="${database.username}"
```

**Example 4-5.** build.xml

```
        password="">
        <classpath>
            <path refid="mysql.class.path"/>
        </classpath>
        <fileset dir="${db.dir}">
            <include name="rentabike.sql"/>
        </fileset>
    </sql>
</target>
```

## What just happened?

You're now set up and ready to put Spring through its paces. You just installed MySQL, the database engine. You started the database service and then created a database, so you know it's working. Since all Java applications will access MySQL through a JDBC driver, you installed one so that our application could find it. Then, you created a new Ant task, and ran the task to create a database and some sample data.

You need to be careful to make sure that both the database and the driver work. These verification steps may seem tedious, but they'll save you a whole lot of time in the long run, because things are much easier to debug before you add additional layers.

## What about...

...HyperSQL, Oracle, DB2, or some other database? You used MySQL because it's one of the most widely used open source databases. Spring will make sure that much of what you're going to do will be portable. If you'd like, you can install any database, as long as you make sure to install a working JDBC driver.

## Using Spring JDBC Templates

Although persistence frameworks like EJB container-managed persistence, JDO, and Hibernate have attracted fans at various times, JDBC remains the bread-and-butter of database development with Java. You can write it all yourself, or you can use some frameworks to help manage the details. Spring lets you do JDBC development in a variety of ways. In this example, you'll use JDBC templates.

If Spring offered nothing more than a little configuration, a smattering of user interface development, and a slightly different programming model, then this book would be done, but Spring offers much more, including tremendous advantages over roll-your-own JDBC:

*Resource management*
> Spring will open and close connections for you, so you won't have to write that tedious code, and you won't have leaks.

*Unchecked exceptions*
> Spring will not force you to use checked exceptions, so you won't have to make those tedious checks for errors that you can't recover from anyway. Instead, you can catch the right exception at the right level.

*Inversion of control*
> Spring will iterate your result set for you, saving effort and keeping your approach consistent.

*Configuration*
> Spring will let you configure and exchange out resources like data sources and connections, without changing code.

In short, you'll write less code, and build programs that are easier to maintain and read. You'll let Spring, instead of tedious, handwritten code do the heavy lifting.

## How do I do that?

Spring uses a concept called templates. You'll pass each template an SQL query, and a method that will process each row in a result set. Normally, that code, in an inner class, will map the results from a query onto objects. Spring will do the rest.

You'll put the template code into an implementation of our façade layer. Since you've already got an interface, a test implementation and the object model for the application, you'll create the JDBC implementation, which extends a Spring-provided class called JdbcDaoSupport that makes life easier (Example 4-6).

**Example 4-6.** JDBCRentABike.java

```
public class JDBCRentABike extends JdbcDaoSupport implements RentABike {
    private String storeName;
    private static final int MANUFACTURER = 2;
    private static final int MODEL = 3;
    private static final int FRAME = 4;
    private static final int SERIALNO = 5;
    private static final int WEIGHT = 6;
    private static final int STATUS = 7;
```

**Example 4-6.** JDBCRentABike.java (continued)

```java
public List getBikes() {
    final ArrayList results = new ArrayList();
    JdbcTemplate template = getJdbcTemplate();
    template.query("SELECT * FROM bikes",
        new RowCallbackHandler() {
            public void processRow(ResultSet rs)
                throws SQLException {
                    Bike bike = new Bike(rs.getString(MANUFACTURER),
                    rs.getString(MODEL), rs.getInt(FRAME),
                    rs.getString(SERIALNO), rs.getDouble(WEIGHT),
                    rs.getString(STATUS));
                    results.add(bike);
                }
        });
    return results;
}

public Bike getBike(String serialNo) {
    final Bike bike = new Bike();
    JdbcTemplate template = getJdbcTemplate();
    template.query("SELECT * FROM bikes WHERE bikes.serialNo = '"
        + serialNo + "'",
        new RowCallbackHandler() {
            public void processRow(ResultSet rs)
                throws SQLException {
                    bike.setManufacturer(rs.getString(MANUFACTURER));
                    bike.setModel(rs.getString(MODEL));
                    bike.setFrame(rs.getInt(FRAME));
                    bike.setSerialNo(rs.getString(SERIALNO));
                    bike.setWeight(rs.getDouble(WEIGHT));
                    bike.setStatus(rs.getString(STATUS));
                }
        });
    return bike;
}

//etc...
```

*This method is provided by JdbcDaoSupport.*

*This code does the bulk of the JDBC work. Think of a template as a default JDBC method. You pass the query, and the code that you want to execute for each record in the result set.*

*You'd probably prefer to pass just a few lines of code, instead of a full inner class. Java doesn't support closures and code blocks like Ruby and Groovy do, so you're stuck with this syntax.*

This may look a bit muddy, until you compare it to a traditional JDBC method. The inner class syntax is a little awkward, but you'll learn it quickly.

Next, add the data source and the JDBC connection to the context. Also, we need to point the application to the new façade implementation (Example 4-7).

**Example 4-7.** RentABikeApp-Servlet.xml

```xml
<bean id="dataSource"
    class="org.springframework.jdbc.datasource.DriverManagerDataSource">
```

This is
dependency
injection in action.
The façade will
have access to the
data source
through its
superclass,
JdbcDaoSupport.

**Example 4-7.** RentABikeApp-Servlet.xml (continued)

```xml
    <property name="driverClassName">
        <value>com.mysql.jdbc.Driver</value>
    </property>
    <property name="url">
        <value>jdbc:mysql://localhost/bikestore</value>
    </property>
    <property name="username"><value>bikestore</value></property>
</bean>

<bean id="rentaBike" class="com.springbook.JDBCRentABike">
    <property name="storeName"><value>Bruce's Bikes</value></property>
    <property name="dataSource"><ref bean="dataSource"/></property>
</bean>
```

Don't forget to wrap any calls to the JdbcTemplate in appropriate error handling. Any time you invoke your own or somebody else's code to access a database, things can go wrong (failed connection, invalid permissions, locked data, etc.). You should have a plan for dealing with these kinds of exceptions and treat any call to the JdbcTemplate as a potential for failure.

## What just happened?

For the code that sits above the façade, you're not seeing much of a difference between the test version and the database version. That's the beauty of the test façade that you built early in Chapter 1. However, now multiple applications can share the database, and it will retain changes between invocations, just as you'd expect.

In the façade, we used a JDBC template. We provide three pieces of data to the JDBC template:

*The query*
    The first parameter specifies a raw query.

*The parameters*
    If the statement is a parameterized query, you can specify all of the variable parameters that the statement requires.

*A callback class*
    We can also specify an inner class, with one method, to match the RowCallbackHandler interface. The method will fire for each line in the result set.

Notice that all of the code that we specify is necessary. These are the things that change from one JDBC invocation to the next. Instead of specifying the control structures (like a while loop) to iterate through the result set, we hand control to Spring. It then does the grunt work:

1. Spring gets a connection from a data source.
2. Spring specifies (and potentially prepares) the SQL statement.
3. Spring then iterates through the result set.
4. For each line in the statement, Spring calls the callback that we specify.
5. Spring then closes down the connection.
6. If there's an exception, Spring folds it to an unchecked, common exception.

But what happened is not nearly as important as how it happened. Go back and read the code in the façade once again. Think again about all of the things that Spring does for us:

*Exception management at low levels*

While there might be some JDBC errors within the façade layer, it's probably not the best place to deal with the problem. Instead, the client of the façade is probably in a much better place to deal with the problem. I'd go as far as saying that checked exceptions in Java were a mistake. Spring helps to rectify that mistake.

*Exception folding*

Databases bury a SQL code into SQLExceptions. Even though this application may run on multiple databases, we don't see the application react in different ways to the different exceptions thrown by different databases. Spring folds exceptions onto a common set.

*Resource management*

We don't have to open or close the connection. The framework does this for us. We don't have to worry about leaks, because the Spring developers have already released the connection appropriately, and tested the results.

*Iteration through the result set*

This is the centerpiece of inversion of control. Spring iterates through the result set, and calls the template for each row in the result set.

*Transactions*

We could simply set the JDBC to auto-commit, as in this example. If we were to change our minds, the application would have to change. Spring lets us specify a transaction strategy in the configuration, as you'll see in Chapter 7.

*Other services*

Spring will let you attach other services to the façade through configuration instead of code.

Figure 4-1 shows the work that nearly all JDBC programs must do. The blocks in grey show the operations that Spring handles for you. You've got to do the rest yourself.

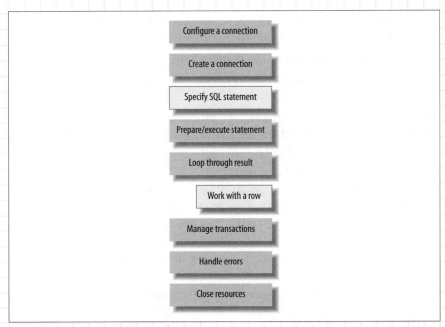

**Figure 4-1.** JDBC requires all of these operations, but Spring handles the ones in grey automatically

## What about...

...persistence frameworks? We introduce a few in the next chapter. With the advent of Hibernate and the resurgence of JDO, you might be convinced that there's never any reason to use JDBC, but remember, you don't need a flamethrower to swat a fly. Like that flamethrower in the living room, your persistence framework may have some unintended consequences. If you've got a flyweight problem, grab a flyswatter.

On the other hand, the previous code tied the object fields to specific database datatypes. If a developer is supporting both Oracle and MySql, and a field might grow longer than Oracle's VARCHAR will handle, it must be defined as a CLOB. JDBC's CLOB handling does not match VAR-CHAR handling at all. MySQL doesn't present this problem. You'd either need to handle the difference yourself, or reach for a more robust persistence solution.

# Refactoring Out Common Code

If you're paying attention, you've probably noticed a little repetition. In fact, some of those inner classes may be better served by separate classes that can populate your domain model. In this example, you'll refactor a little of that common code.

Your small objects may keep this book short, but they're not particularly realistic. Business objects typically have many more fields. If you try to do everything in line, you can accumulate a little too much replication. I like repetition about as much as I like paddling on flat water. In fact, my worst injuries have both come on easier rapids, or easy trails, because I wasn't not paying attention as closely as I should have been. You're likely to find the same phenomenon with tedious, repetitive code: the monotony can keep you from paying attention, and cause an uncomfortable number of minor injuries.

## How do I do that?

You're simply going to break some of the code in those inner classes free, so they're easier to read and easier to reuse. You'll focus on the code that populates each object (Example 4-8).

**Example 4-8.** JDBCRentABike.java

```
public List getBikes() {
    final ArrayList results = new ArrayList();
    JdbcTemplate template = new JdbcTemplate();

    class BikesHandler implements RowCallbackHandler {
        public void processRow(ResultSet rs) throws SQLException {
            Bike bike = new Bike(rs.getString(MANUFACTURER),
            rs.getString(MODEL), rs.getInt(FRAME), rs.getString(SERIALNO),
            rs.getDouble(WEIGHT), rs.getString(STATUS));
            results.add(bike);
        }
    }
    template.query("SELECT * FROM bikes", new BikesHandler());
    return results;
}

public Bike getBike(String serialNo) {
    final Bike bike = new Bike();
    JdbcTemplate template = new JdbcTemplate();
    class BikeHandler implements RowCallbackHandler {
        public void processRow(ResultSet rs) throws SQLException {
        bike.setManufacturer(rs.getString(MANUFACTURER));
        bike.setModel(rs.getString(MODEL));
        bike.setFrame(rs.getInt(FRAME));
```

*This handler is still an inner class, but it's a named inner class. This tool is useful for improving readability, but still maintaining all of the code for a DAO or other object in a single file.*

**Example 4-8.** JDBCRentABike.java (continued)

```
    bike.setSerialNo(rs.getString(SERIALNO));
    bike.setWeight(rs.getDouble(WEIGHT));
    bike.setStatus(rs.getString(STATUS));
    }
  }

  template.query("SELECT * FROM bikes WHERE bikes.serialNo = '"
    + serialNo + "'", new BikeHandler());

  return bike;
}
```

When you run the application, you should get the same behavior, since once again, you're only changing database logic. Notice how Spring is protecting the user interface from churn.

## What just happened?

The execution path is the same. You just replaced the in-line inner classes with named inner classes. The result is practically identical execution, but with a cleaner code base.

# Using Access Objects

In this example, you're going to take a simple query object and wrap it up in a reusable form. Spring provides an API called *RDBMS operational objects* to help you wrap stored procedures, queries, and updates.

You may find that you're repetitively defining a block of SQL or a stored procedure. Wrapping it up into a reusable form adds convenience and clarity to your code. Plus, you'll create a thread-safe, reusable form.

## How do I do that?

In this case, you'll use this feature to look for reservations. To do so, create a new MappingSqlQuery class for each kind of reservation search. Specify parameters for each of the parameters of the query, and then set the types for each of the parameters. As before, you'll specify a method to map each row, with an inner class. Example 4-9 shows the code we have so far.

**Example 4-9.** JDBCRentABike.java

```
abstract class FindReservations extends MappingSqlQuery {
  protected List reservations = new ArrayList();
```

**Example 4-9.** JDBCRentABike.java (continued)

```java
    protected FindReservations(DataSource dataSource, String query) {
        super(dataSource, query);
    }

    protected Object mapRow(ResultSet rs, int rownum)
            throws SQLException {
        int resId = rs.getInt(1);
        int bikeId = rs.getInt(2);
        int custId = rs.getInt(3);
        Date resDate = rs.getDate(4);

        Bike bike = getBike(bikeId);
        Customer customer = getCustomer(custId);
        Reservation reservation = new Reservation(resId, bike,
            customer, resDate);
        reservations.add(reservation);
        return reservation;
    }

    abstract List findReservations(int param);
}

class FindReservationsByCustomer extends FindReservations {
    public FindReservationsByCustomer(DataSource dataSource) {
        super(dataSource,
            "SELECT * FROM reservations WHERE custId = ?");
        declareParameter(new SqlParameter(Types.INTEGER));
        compile();
    }

    public List findReservations(int param) {
        execute(param);
        return this.reservations;
    }
}

class FindReservationsByBike extends FindReservations {
    public FindReservationsByBike(DataSource dataSource) {
        super(dataSource,
            "SELECT * FROM reservations WHERE bikeId = ?");
        declareParameter(new SqlParameter(Types.INTEGER));
        compile();
    }

    public List findReservations(int param) {
        execute(param);
        return reservations;
    }
}
```

*This method simply maps a row onto an object. The RDBMS objects formalize this method.*

*Here's where you set the query.*

You can use the new query whenever you need to query for appointments, as in Example 4-10.

**Example 4-10.** JDBCRentABike.java

```java
public List getReservations(Customer customer) {
        return new FindReservationsByCustomer(dataSource).
            findReservations(customer.getCustId());
    }

    public List getReservations(Bike bike) {
        return new FindReservationsByBike(dataSource).
            findReservations(bike.getBikeId());
    }
```

You'll run the code as before.

At this point, you will also add two new domain classes that represent customers and reservations.

**Example 4-11.** Customer.java

```java
package com.springbook;
import java.util.Set;

public class Customer {
    private int custId;
    private String firstName;
    private String lastName;
    private Set reservations;

    public Set getReservations() { return reservations; }

    public void setReservations(Set reservations)
        { this.reservations = reservations; }

    public int getCustId() { return custId; }

    public void setCustId(int custId) { this.custId = custId; }

    public String getFirstName() { return firstName; }

    public void setFirstName(String firstName) { this.firstName = firstName; }

    public String getLastName() { return lastName; }

    public void setLastName(String lastName) { this.lastName = lastName;}

    public Customer(int custId, String firstName, String lastName) {
        this.CustId = custId;
        this.firstName = firstName;
        this.lastName = lastName;
    }

    public Customer() {}

    public String toString() {
        return "Customer : " +
```

**Example 4-11.** Customer.java

```
            "custId -- " + custId +
            "\n: firstName --" + firstName +
            "\n: lastName --" + lastName +
            ".\n";
    }
}
```

**Example 4-12.** Reservation.java

```java
package com.springbook;
import java.util.Date;

public class Reservation {
    private int reservationId;
    private Date reservationDate;
    private Bike bike;
    private Customer customer;

    public Reservation() {}

    public int getReservationId() { return reservationId; }

    public void setReservationId(int reservationId)
        { this.reservationId = reservationId; }

    public Date getReservationDate() { return reservationDate; }

    public void setReservationDate(Date reservationDate)
        { this.reservationDate = reservationDate; }

    public Bike getBike() { return bike; }

    public void setBike(Bike bike) { this.bike = bike; }

    public Customer getCustomer() { return customer;}

    public void setCustomer(Customer customer) { this.customer = customer; }

    public Reservation(int id, Bike bike, Customer customer, Date date) {
        this.reservationId = id;
        this.bike = bike;
        this.customer = customer;
        this.reservationDate = date;
    }

    public String toString() {
        return "Reservation : " +
            "reservationId -- " + reservationId +
            "\n: reservationDate -- " + reservationDate +
            "\n: bike -- " + bike +
```

**Example 4-12.** Reservation.java

```
        "\n: customer -- " + customer +
        ".\n";
    }
}
```

## What just happened?

You created a reusable, parameterized package. It's clean and simple. The MapRow method converts each row of the data set into an object. The query then returns a list of bikes in the store that will fit criteria we specify. You created an object hierarchy to allow for two different kinds of reservation queries; to add more (search by date, by customer and date, etc.), you just need to make more subclasses of FindReservations.

## What about...

...stored procedures? Most object-heads despise stored procedures, but they're part of the landscape in many places. You can't just hide your head in the sand. Placing a stored procedure in a cleaner object oriented package that maps the results into objects certainly can make them more palatable.

I'll go a step farther. While stored procedures do not provide the cleanest or most elegant code, you can and should use them for spot performance optimizations. A stored procedure can often reduce round trips to the database by more than an order of magnitude. I can recall a performance benchmark that compared DB2 with a set of other databases. My team noticed that DB2 was slower by a factor of eight behind one of our rivals. After several late nights and a few rolls of Tums, we noticed that the benchmarking testing company had used stored procedures for the competition, but not DB2. When the testing laboratory reran the tests, DB2 was once again on top. You don't have to go crazy with them, but never underestimate stored procedures when you're spot-tuning and none of the quicker optimizations are working.

## Running a Test with EasyMock

It's time to run a test case. Since you're testing a JDBC application, it makes sense for us to verify that it's been used correctly.

Let's say that you wanted to test a single turn signal, one time. One way would be to stand behind the car, and then have someone inside activate the signal. If it didn't blink, then you'd say so. But say that you wanted to test the device before you put it into a car. One strategy would be to plug in a volt meter, a device that measures electricity, instead of a light bulb. Then, if the signal did not generate the right amount of electricity at the right time, the test would fail.

That's how a mock object works. Sometimes, instead of simulating the real world (like our stub in Chapter 1 that simulated a database), you want to know how your object under test is using its interfaces. You might use a mock object instead of a JDBC interface to make sure that the application opens the connection and closes it, just as you expect.

## How do I do that?

You'll first need to install EasyMock. Download the latest version from *http://www.easymock.org* and place the *easymock.jar* file in your project's classpath. We've added it to our */lib* folder.

Next, you can establish the collection of mock objects you'll need (Example 4-13). You are effectively drilling down through the JDBC interfaces, and it turns out you will use four of them.

**Example 4-13.** ControllerTest.java

```java
public void testGetBikesWithMocks( ) throws Exception {
    DataSource mockDataSource;
    Connection mockConnection;
    Statement mockStatement;
    ResultSet mockRS;

    MockControl controlDataSource =
        MockControl.createControl(DataSource.class);
    MockControl controlConnection =
        MockControl.createNiceControl(Connection.class);
    MockControl controlStatement =
        MockControl.createControl(Statement.class);
    MockControl controlRS =
        MockControl.createControl(ResultSet.class);
            mockDataSource = (DataSource)controlDataSource.getMock( );
            mockConnection = (Connection)controlConnection.getMock( );
            mockStatement = (Statement)controlStatement.getMock( );
            mockRS = (ResultSet)controlRS.getMock( );
```

Next, you will set the expectations. Using EasyMock, you do this by recording a working version of your intended test case. When you do the record, you're telling EasyMock how the application should behave (Example 4-14).

**Example 4-14.** ControllerTest.java

```
mockDataSource.getConnection();
controlDataSource.setReturnValue(mockConnection);

mockConnection.createStatement();
controlConnection.setReturnValue(mockStatement);

mockStatement.executeQuery("SELECT * FROM bikes");
controlStatement.setReturnValue(mockRS);

controlRS.expectAndReturn(mockRS.next(), false);

controlStatement.expectAndReturn(mockStatement.getWarnings(),
    null);

mockRS.close();
mockStatement.close();
mockConnection.close();
```

Next, you'll play the test case back, as in Example 4-15.

**Example 4-15.** ControllerTest.java

```
controlConnection.replay();
controlDataSource.replay();
controlStatement.replay();
controlRS.replay();
```

Finally, you will kick off the actual test and verify the test case (Example 4-16). If the verification step fails, then the test case will fail, just as if an assertion failed in basic JUnit.

**Example 4-16.** ControllerTest.java

```
JDBCRentABike jstore = (JDBCRentABike)store;
jstore.setDataSource(mockDataSource);
List bikes = store.getBikes();

controlConnection.verify();
controlDataSource.verify();
controlStatement.verify();
controlRS.verify();
```

Let's say that you forgot to record the ResultSet being closed (by leaving out the call mockRS.close()). Example 4-17 shows the results of running the unit test.

**Example 4-17.** Output from running ControllerTest.java

```
junit.framework.AssertionFailedError:
  Unexpected method call close():
    close(): expected: 0, actual: 1
```

**Example 4-17.** *Output from running ControllerTest.java (continued)*

```
    at org.easymock.internal.ObjectMethodsFilter.invoke(ObjectMethodsFilter.java:44)
    at $Proxy3.close(Unknown Source)
    at org.springframework.jdbc.support.JdbcUtils.closeResultSet(JdbcUtils.java:69)
    at org.springframework.jdbc.core.JdbcTemplate$1QueryStatementCallback.
doInStatement(JdbcTemplate.java:259)
    at org.springframework.jdbc.core.JdbcTemplate.execute(JdbcTemplate.java:204)
    at org.springframework.jdbc.core.JdbcTemplate.query(JdbcTemplate.java:266)
    at org.springframework.jdbc.core.JdbcTemplate.query(JdbcTemplate.java:270)
    at com.springbook.JDBCRentABike.getBikes(JDBCRentABike.java:56)
    at JDBCFacadeTest.testGetBikesWithMocks(JDBCFacadeTest.java:75)
    at sun.reflect.NativeMethodAccessorImpl.invoke0(Native Method)
    at sun.reflect.NativeMethodAccessorImpl.invoke(NativeMethodAccessorImpl.java:39)
    at sun.reflect.DelegatingMethodAccessorImpl.
invoke(DelegatingMethodAccessorImpl.java:25)
    at com.intellij.rt.execution.junit2.JUnitStarter.main(Unknown Source)
```

# What just happened?

You've seen dynamic mock objects in action. The nice thing about dynamic mock objects is that you can test sophisticated user interfaces, like JDBC, without having to simulate all of its behavior.

# What about...

...other mock object frameworks? You don't have to use EasyMock. Other mock object frameworks work as well. The overall flow is the same. For any framework, we'll see the following steps (similar to the ones described in the sidebar above):

*Set the expectations for success*
>  A mock object will replace one or more interfaces in an application. It doesn't need to act like the real thing, but it does need to simulate the input and output.

*Exercise the mock object*
>  You'll make the object under test do something.

*Verify the mock object*
>  You'll then ask the mock object if it was used in the way that you expected.

For some, mock objects might seem to be awkward. Stay with them, and you'll learn to appreciate how they ease your testing burden. Just don't throw away everything else in your toolbox to make room for this, or any other, golden hammer.

You have just seen how to use simple JDBC with Spring. In the next chapter, you'll see how Spring can do many of the same things for other persistence solutions, including full object relational frameworks.

# Stubs and Mocks

In Chapter 2, we used an array list instead of a database. Many programmers mistakenly think that this technique is called mocking. Actually, that's not quite true. A stub simulates a real-world scenario, like the array list simulates a database. The stub seeks to make your application lighter, so that it will be easier to run, test, and build: while you're working on other parts of the system, you don't have to keep the database running.

Mock objects are different. Their job is to measure the way an interface is used. You'd use a mock object to verify that a connection gets closed, or that the right query gets called in the first place. When you use a mock strategy, you'll have three distinct steps:

*Set expectations*
> This step has two purposes. First, your object must work with the application in the same way that the real-world code works with the application. While it doesn't have to simulate real-world side effects, it needs to return a correct value. The second part of this step is to define the right stream of calls, including the right parameters and the right order. For example, your expectation step could open a connection, run a query, return a hardcoded result set, and close the connection.

*Use the mock object in test conditions*
> This step records the way your application actually uses the mock API.

*Verify the results*
> This step compares the expectations against the actual use. If they are the same, the test passes. Otherwise, the test fails.

Which is better? That depends on what you need to do. Use stubs to replace heavyweight real-world implementations—for example, to test a user interface without needing a full database. Make certain test cases shorter. Use mocks to verify the use of an API. Mocks are very good at making sure that cleanup happens correctly, and that APIs are used correctly.

# OR Persistence

Near where I live, there's a notorious mountain biking trail with a hill called Beer Mountain. I have no idea how it got its name, because you've got to be stone-cold sober to even contemplate going down. As far as I know, it's never been cleanly climbed (or climbed without stepping off of the bike). Most think it's ridiculous to even try. The hill is long and has an insanely steep gradient. It's covered with loose rock and lots of ledges. I must be too bored with the rest of my life, because I've been working to climb that hill for two and a half years. A hill like that one looks to me like a difficult programming problem. I have started over many times, trying different approaches to the many ledges and boulder gardens on the way to the top. To climb Beer Mountain, I needed to improve my bike, my technique, and my conditioning.

Object-relational mapping has been that type of problem for Java developers. We needed a combination of processing power, better design patterns, and better persistence frameworks to make cleaner persistence designs solvable. We're finally starting to make real progress. Now, we're nearing the top of this hill, and frameworks like Spring are part of the equation, because they make ORM do more with less effort. In this chapter, you'll see three frameworks: iBATIS, JDO, and Hibernate:

- iBATIS is a JDBC helper framework that gives you some of the benefits of OR mapping and usage, but without as much risk.

- JDO is an embattled persistence standard, but with a couple of exceptional implementations that are among the most polished persistence frameworks in the industry.

- Hibernate is an open source persistence framework, under control of the JBoss group. It's probably the most popular persistence framework right now. Large customers adopt it with increasing regularity.

In this chapter, you'll work with all three, without changing any code for the rest of the application!

# Integrating iBATIS

In a fiasco that's become famous, a sample application from Sun was used as a centerpiece for a benchmark in a widely publicized competition between J2EE and .NET. The .NET version soundly beat the EJB-based J2EE version, and the heat was on. Clinton Begin built a simplified version of PetStore around his persistence framework called iBATIS, and it's grown in popularity ever since. Spring provides excellent iBATIS integration, and we'll look at it in this chapter.

Not all problems are well-suited for full-blown persistence frameworks. They're moderately complicated in the best of circumstances. Without the right skills or with an inappropriate problem, they can be disastrous. In a class that we teach together, Ted Neward, the author of Effective Enterprise Java, often compares building or adopting a persistence framework to the United States war in Vietnam, claiming that they're both seductive wars to enter, but both wars are difficult to win, and there's no effective exit strategy in either case. You can still find the blog at *http://www.neward.net*.

While I won't go quite that far, it's nice to have a framework like iBATIS SqlMaps that gives you a taste of an OR usage model without forcing you to eat a whole elephant with one bite. Specifically, iBATIS lets you:

- Map columns and SQL statements to keywords
- Use the full power of SQL without the tedium of JDBC
- Break your SQL away from your code

Spring with iBATIS gives you these advantages and more. Let's get busy.

## How do I do that?

First, you need to install iBATIS. You don't have to configure it right away, because the configuration will go into your Spring application context. You can find it at *http://www.ibatis.com/*. Download it and set it up. We're using Version 1.3.1 for this book. Place the iBATIS-provided jars (*ibatis-sqlmap.jar*, *ibatis-dao.jar*, and *ibatis-common.jar*) as well as the Spring-provided *jdom.jar* (in Spring's */lib* folder) in the */war/WEB-INF/lib* folder of your *project* directory).

You've already got the interface for the façade and the model, so you need an implementation of the façade and the SQL statements. First, you can implement the façade for the application, as in Example 5-1.

**Example 5-1.** IBatisRentABike.java

```java
public class IBatisRentABike extends SqlMapDaoSupport
    implements RentABike {

    private String storeName = "";

    public void setStoreName(String name) {this.storeName = name;}
    public String getStoreName() {return this.storeName;}


    public List getBikes() {
        return getSqlMapTemplate().executeQueryForList("getBikes", null);
    }

    public Bike getBike(String serialNo) {
        return (Bike) getSqlMapTemplate().
            executeQueryForObject("getBikeBySerialNo", serialNo);
    }

    public Bike getBike(int bikeId) {
        return (Bike) getSqlMapTemplate().
            executeQueryForObject("getBikeByID", new Integer(bikeId));
    }

    public void saveBike(Bike bike) {
        getSqlMapTemplate().executeUpdate("saveBike", bike);
    }

    public void deleteBike(Bike bike) {
        getSqlMapTemplate().executeUpdate("deleteBike", bike);
    }

    public List getCustomers() {
        return getSqlMapTemplate().
            executeQueryForList("getCustomers", null);
    }

    public Customer getCustomer(int custId) {
        return (Customer) getSqlMapTemplate().
            executeQueryForObject("getCustomer", new Integer(custId));
    }

    public List getReservations() {
        return getSqlMapTemplate().
            executeQueryForList("getReservations", null);
    }
```

*These are named queries. iBATIS breaks each query out into a separate map and lets you execute them by name.*

**Example 5-1.** IBatisRentABike.java (continued)

```java
    public List getReservations(Customer customer) {
        return getSqlMapTemplate().
            executeQueryForList("getReservationsForCustomer", customer);
    }

    public List getReservations(Bike bike) {
        return getSqlMapTemplate().
            executeQueryForList("getReservationsForBike", bike);
    }

    public List getReservations(Date date) {
        return getSqlMapTemplate().
            executeQueryForList("getReservationsForDate", date);
    }

    public Reservation getReservation(int resId) {
        return (Reservation) getSqlMapTemplate().
            executeQueryForObject("getReservation", new Integer(resId));
    }
}
```

The `SqlMapTemplate` is provided by Spring's `SqlMapDaoSupport` class which our `RentABike` implementation must extend. It handles the establishment and management of connections to the underlying data store as well as interpretation of the map files you provide. You can look at the template as a default implementation for the things you'd like to do with an iBATIS named query.

You'll also need to create the SQL statements. You can give each SQL statement a name. Then, you'll map the results to a Java bean. You have two choices here. You can either reference every bean property in an SQL AS alias, or build an explicit map between the query and the bean, as in Example 5-2. Also included here are the mappings for *Customer* and *Reservation* as well.

**Example 5-2.** Bike.xml (an IBatis SQL map file)

```xml
<?xml version="1.0" encoding="UTF-8"?>
<!DOCTYPE sql-map
    PUBLIC "-//iBATIS.com//DTD SQL Map 1.0//EN"
    "http://www.ibatis.com/dtd/sql-map.dtd">

<sql-map name="Bike">

  <result-map name="result" class="com.springbook.Bike">
    <property name="bikeId" column="bikeId" columnIndex="1"/>
    <property name="manufacturer" column="manufacturer" columnIndex="2"/>
    <property name="model" column="model" columnIndex="3"/>
    <property name="frame" column="frame" columnIndex="4"/>
    <property name="serialNo" column="serialNo" columnIndex="5"/>
```

**Example 5-2.** Bike.xml (an IBatis SQL map file) (continued)

```xml
      <property name="weight" column="weight" columnIndex="6"/>
      <property name="status" column="status" columnIndex="7"/>
  </result-map>

  <mapped-statement name="getBikes" result-map="result">
    select bikeId, manufacturer, model, frame, serialNo, weight, status
    from bikes
  </mapped-statement>

  <mapped-statement name="getBikeBySerialNo" result-map="result">
    select bikeId, manufacturer, model, frame, serialNo, weight, status
    from bikes
    where serialNo=#value#
  </mapped-statement>

  <mapped-statement name="getBikeByID" result-map="result">
    select bikeId, manufacturer, model, frame, serialNo, weight, status
    from bikes
    where bikeId=#value#
  </mapped-statement>

  <mapped-statement name="saveBike">
    insert into bikes
      (bikeId, manufacturer, model, frame, serialNo, weight, status)
      values (#bikeId#, #manufacturer#, #model#, #frame#, #serialNo#,
      #weight#, #status#)
  </mapped-statement>

  <mapped-statement name="deleteBike">
      delete from bikes
      where bikeId = #bikeId#
  </mapped-statement>
</sql-map>
```

**Example 5-3.** Customer.xml

```xml
<?xml version="1.0" encoding="UTF-8"?>
<!DOCTYPE sql-map
    PUBLIC "-//iBATIS.com//DTD SQL Map 1.0//EN"
    "http://www.ibatis.com/dtd/sql-map.dtd">

<sql-map name="Customer">

    <result-map name="result" class="com.springbook.Customer">
        <property name="custId" column="custId" columnIndex="1"/>
        <property name="firstName" column="firstname" columnIndex="2"/>
        <property name="lastName" column="lastname" columnIndex="3"/>
    </result-map>

    <mapped-statement name="getCustomers" result-map="result">
      select
          custId,
```

**Example 5-3.** Customer.xml

```
            firstname,
            lastname
        from customers
    </mapped-statement>

    <mapped-statement name="getCustomer" result-map="result">
        select
            custId,
            firstname,
            lastname,
        from customers
        where custId = #value#
    </mapped-statement>
</sql-map>
```

**Example 5-4.** Reservation.xml

```
<?xml version="1.0" encoding="UTF-8"?>
<!DOCTYPE sql-map
    PUBLIC "-//iBATIS.com//DTD SQL Map 1.0//EN"
    "http://www.ibatis.com/dtd/sql-map.dtd">

<sql-map name="Reservation">

    <result-map name="result" class="com.springbook.Reservation">
        <property name="reservationId" column="resId" columnIndex="1"/>
        <property name="bike" column="bikeId" columnIndex="2"/>
        <property name="customer" column="custId" columnIndex="3"/>
        <property name="reservationDate" column="resDate" columnIndex="4"/>
    </result-map>

    <mapped-statement name="getReservations" result-map="result">
        select
            resId,
            bikeId,
            custId,
            resDate
        from reservations
    </mapped-statement>

    <mapped-statement name="getReservationsForCustomer" result-map="result">
        select
            resId,
            bikeId,
            custId,
            resDate
        from reservations
        where custId = #value#
    </mapped-statement>
```

**Example 5-4.** Reservation.xml

```xml
<mapped-statement name="getReservationsForBike" result-map="result">
    select
        resId,
        bikeId,
        custId,
        resDate
    from reservations
    where bikeId = #value#
</mapped-statement>

<mapped-statement name="getReservationsForDate" result-map="result">
    select
        resId,
        bikeId,
        custId,
        resDate
    from reservations
    where resDate = #value#
</mapped-statement>

<mapped-statement name="getReservation" result-map="result">
    select
        resId,
        bikeId,
        custId,
        resDate
    from reservations
    where resId = #value#
</mapped-statement>
</sql-map>
```

The `<result-map>` portion provides an explicit map between columns in the database and properties of a persistent class. The `<mapped-statements>` can then simply define the SQL queries necessary to execute the needed functionality, and the map handles creation of the resultant Java object. In addition to the `Bike` version above, your application currently also requires a map for `Customer` and `Reservation`.

You're going to have to do a little work that an OR framework would normally do for us, like create identifiers. In this case, you're going to use MySQL sequences (which are just `AUTO_INCREMENT` columns on a table). You simply define our table with the `bikeId` column marked as `AUTO_INCREMENT` and, when inserting a new row, ignore the `bikeId` column. The `SaveBike` statement from our map now becomes Example 5-5.

**Example 5-5.** Bike.xml

```xml
<mapped-statement name="saveBike">
   insert into bikes
   (manufacturer, model, frame, serialNo, weight, status)
   values (#manufacturer#, #model#, #frame#, #serialNo#, #weight#,
   #status#)
</mapped-statement>
```

If you are using Oracle, Spring and iBatis support Oracle sequences as well.

Next, you can update the application context. You'll need to specify our new façade, which requires the SQL maps. Introduce the SQL maps in a properties file, like we do the JDBC parameters. You'll also need to configure a transaction strategy (Example 5-6).

**Example 5-6.** RentABikeApp-servlet.xml

```xml
<beans>
   <bean id="dataSource"
      class="org.springframework.jdbc.datasource.DriverManagerDataSource">
      <property name="driverClassName">
         <value>com.mysql.jdbc.Driver</value>
      </property>
      <property name="url">
         <value>jdbc:mysql://localhost/bikestore</value>
      </property>
      <property name="username">
         <value>bikestore</value>
      </property>
   </bean>

   <bean id="rentaBike" class="com.springbook.IBatisRentABike">
      <property name="storeName"><value>Bruce's Bikes</value></property>
      <property name="dataSource"><ref local="dataSource"/></property>
      <property name="sqlMap"><ref local="sqlMap"/></property>
   </bean>

   <bean id="sqlMap"
      class="org.springframework.orm.ibatis.SqlMapFactoryBean">
      <property name="configLocation">
         <value>/WEB-INF/ibatis.config</value>
      </property>
   </bean>

   <bean id="transactionManager"
      class="org.springframework.jdbc.datasource.DataSourceTransactionManager">
      <property name="dataSource"><ref local="dataSource"/></property>
   </bean>
```

**Example 5-7.** ibatis.config

```xml
<?xml version="1.0" encoding="UTF-8"?>
<!DOCTYPE sql-map-config
    PUBLIC "-//iBATIS.com//DTD SQL Map Config 1.0//EN"
    "http://www.ibatis.com/dtd/sql-map-config.dtd">
<sql-map-config>
    <sql-map resource="Bike.xml" />
    <sql-map resource="Customer.xml" />
    <sql-map resource="Reservation.xml" />
</sql-map-config>
```

We'll talk about the transaction strategy more later.

## What just happened?

You're not seeing OR mapping. An OR framework will typically tie a data-base *table* to a class, or classes. In this case, iBATIS attaches the results from a *query* to a class. That means that iBATIS makes no attempt to hide SQL from you at all. In fact, it embraces SQL.

Spring is going to simplify iBATIS usage through templates. The iBATIS template will give you a similar usage model to the JDBC template. You'll specify a datasource and an iBATIS mapped SQL statement.

When you execute the statement, Spring works with iBATIS to manage the resources for you, creating and closing connections as required. Spring will pass the mapped statement to iBATIS, which executes the mapped statement, and if necessary, puts the result set into the bean that you specified when you mapped the SQL statement. If you've got any parameters, you place those in a hash map and pass those to the template with the mapped statement.

While the internals might not look like an OR framework, the usage model definitely has an OR flavor to it. Build data access objects with methods to manipulate the data store. You don't see SQL in your code; it remains in configuration files. Work with collections of objects instead of result sets. In short, it's an elegant compromise between full OR and JDBC.

## What about...

...using iBATIS for everything? Since this usage model is so similar to an OR model and since many applications need more control over the SQL that they might generate, you may be tempted to use iBATIS pervasively. Still, there's room for OR frameworks like JDO and Hibernate. OR frameworks give you more flexibility and power:

*This transaction strategy is in the context. You won't have to manage commits, because Spring will do those for you. You'll see a more complete treatment of transactions in Chapter 6.*

- Some advanced object models lead to very complex SQL, which is best delivered through ORM. For example, inheritance often complicates native JDBC.

- Some advanced performance features, like lazy loading and fetch groups, require a more formal model for effective automation. While perfectly tuned JDBC will always be at least as fast as ORM, the performance tuning options afforded by ORM make it easier to get better performance for some types of problems than native JDBC.

- ORM makes some problems less tedious. It's simply easier to manipulate an object than to create a set of SQL queries. Applications with simple finders and create, update, read-by-primary-key, and delete may be easier with ORM.

If you have a rapidly changing data model and object model, iBATIS can come up short. If you've got a CRUD style application, then iBATIS may be a little tedious for you. If, instead, you're looking for good access to SQL and an effective compromise between ORM and native JDBC, then iBATIS can probably give you everything you need.

# Using Spring with JDO

JDO is the non-EJB standard for persistence in Java applications. In this section, we'll use our favorite JDO implementation, Kodo, to implement transparent persistence for our application. In this section, I'm not going to try to teach you JDO, but I will show you how to use it to provide persistence to our application.

If you've followed JDO for any length of time, it probably brings to mind all sorts of feverish battles with the intensity of the Crusades. Until recently, most people avoided JDO. With the pending release of JDO 2.0 and several solid commercial and open source JDO implementations, this persistence standard seems to be gathering momentum as a stronger player in the ORM space. In fact, my favorite ORM implementation is Solar Metric's Kodo, possibly the leading JDO implementation. It seems to be more robust than the alternatives when it comes to commercial implementations. It's got more flexible mapping support, it's easier to manage, and it's got far richer support for hardcore enterprise persistence. Consider these advantages:

- You can choose between a variety of open source JDO implementations if you're looking for something that's free, or better control of the source code.

- You can choose a commercial implementation, and get support and maintenance for a reasonable price if you don't.

- With the top commercial vendors, you get incredible power and performance, from better management to flexible mapping.
- You get all of this with the protection and security that an open standard provides.

## How do I do that?

You'll use JDO to create a persistent model, and then use that model through a façade layer. The application already has a business domain model created. It's not yet persistent, though. You've also got the interface for the façade layer. You need only do the following steps to enable our application for JDO:

1. Make the domain model persistent. Do that through the byte code enhancer.

2. Configure Spring to use Kodo by making a few simple changes in the configuration file.

3. Build a façade that uses a persistent model through the JDO templates.

That's it. Spring will manage the core JDO resources, consisting of the PersistenceManagerFactory and the PersistenceManager. Think of these special options as the data source and connection for JDO. You can let Spring manage transactions. The three steps above are all that you need.

First, you need to download and install Kodo. Start with the trial version, which you can find at *http://www.solarmetric.com*. You can use Version 3.2.1 for this book. Once again, you have to add the libraries found in */kodo-jdo-3.2.1/lib* to our */lib* folder.

To make the model persistent, modify the Ant task to add JDO's byte code enhancement step: add an Ant task to do so, like in Example 5-8.

**Example 5-8.** build.xml

```
<taskdef name="jdoc" classname="kodo.ant.JDOEnhancerTask"/>

<target name="jdo.enhance">
    <jdoc>
            <fileset dir="${src.dir}">
                    <include name="**/*.jdo" />
            </fileset>
    </jdoc>
</target>
```

You'll also add path elements to your Ant build file for *kodo-jdo.jar, jdo-1.0.1.jar,* and *jakarta-commons-lang-1.0.1.jar*.

Next, build the persistence mapping. The easiest way is through Kodo's wizard. Launch the Workbench (in the \bin directory of your Kodo install) and choose MetaData → Create MetaData from the menu. Conversely, you can use the metadatatool and mappingtool scripts that can be found in /kodo-jdo-3.2.1/bin, which are just launchers for kodo.jdbc.meta. MappingTool and kodo.meta.JDOMetaDataTool, respectively.

To keep things consistent with other JDO versions, though, you're going to build a mapping from scratch, with XML. Generate a .jdo file with our class metadata as well as a .mapping file. Both files reside in the /war/ WEB-INF/classes/com/springbook folder.

Example 5-9 shows the metadata file.

**Example 5-9.** package.jdo

```
<?xml version="1.0" encoding="UTF-8"?>
<jdo>
    <package name="com.springbook">
        <class name="Bike">
            <extension vendor-name="kodo" key="detachable" value="true"/>
            <field name="reservations">
                <collection element-type="Reservation"/>
                <extension vendor-name="kodo" key="inverse-owner" value="bike"/>
                <extension vendor-name="kodo" key="element-dependent"
                    value="true"/>
            </field>
        </class>
        <class name="Customer">
            <extension vendor-name="kodo" key="detachable" value="true"/>
            <field name="reservations">
                <collection element-type="com.springbook.Reservation"/>
                <extension vendor-name="kodo" key="inverse-owner"
                    value="customer"/>
                <extension vendor-name="kodo" key="element-dependent"
                    value="true"/>
            </field>
        </class>
        <class name="Reservation">
            <extension vendor-name="kodo" key="detachable" value="true"/>
        </class>
    </package>
</jdo>
```

Example 5-10 shows the mapping file.

**Example 5-10.** package.mapping

```
<?xml version="1.0" encoding="UTF-8"?>
<mapping>
    <package name="com.springbook">
        <class name="Bike">
            <jdbc-class-map type="base" pk-column="BIKEID" table="BIKES"/>
```

**Example 5-10.** package.mapping (continued)

```
        <field name="bikeId">
           <jdbc-field-map type="value" column="BIKEID"/>
        </field>
        <field name="frame">
           <jdbc-field-map type="value" column="FRAME"/>
        </field>
        <field name="manufacturer">
           <jdbc-field-map type="value" column="MANUFACTURER"/>
        </field>
        <field name="model">
           <jdbc-field-map type="value" column="MODEL"/>
        </field>
        <field name="reservations" default-fetch-group="true">
           <jdbc-field-map type="one-many" ref-column.BIKEID="BIKEID"
              table="RESERVATIONS"/>
        </field>
        <field name="serialNo">
           <jdbc-field-map type="value" column="SERIALNO"/>
        </field>
        <field name="status">
           <jdbc-field-map type="value" column="STATUS"/>
        </field>
        <field name="weight">
           <jdbc-field-map type="value" column="WEIGHT"/>
        </field>
     </class>
     <class name="Customer">
        <jdbc-class-map type="base" pk-column="CUSTID"
           table="CUSTOMERS"/>
        <field name="custId">
           <jdbc-field-map type="value" column="CUSTID"/>
        </field>
        <field name="firstName">
           <jdbc-field-map type="value" column="FIRSTNAME"/>
        </field>
        <field name="lastName">
           <jdbc-field-map type="value" column="LASTNAME"/>
        </field>
        <field name="reservations" default-fetch-group="true">
           <jdbc-field-map type="one-many" ref-column.CUSTID="CUSTID"
              table="RESERVATIONS"/>
        </field>
     </class>
     <class name="Reservation">
        <jdbc-class-map type="base" pk-column="RESID"
           table="RESERVATIONS"/>
        <field name="bike">
           <jdbc-field-map type="one-one" column.BIKEID="BIKEID"/>
        </field>
        <field name="customer">
           <jdbc-field-map type="one-one" column.CUSTID="CUSTID"/>
        </field>
```

**Example 5-10.** package.mapping (continued)

```
        <field name="reservationDate">
           <jdbc-field-map type="value" column="RESDATE"/>
        </field>
        <field name="reservationId">
           <jdbc-field-map type="value" column="RESID"/>
        </field>
     </class>
   </package>
</mapping>
```

It's almost too easy. There's no persistence in the model itself, and that's why you use OR technologies. Still, you'll need a layer of code to use that persistence model for your application. That's the façade layer. You'll see a series of calls to the template. Specify the JDO query language statements for the finders, and the objects to persist for deletes, updates, and inserts. You've already got an interface, but we still need to implement the façade (Example 5-11).

**Example 5-11.** KodoRentABike.java

```
public class KodoRentABike extends JdoDaoSupport implements RentABike {
    private String storeName;

    public List getBikes() {
        return (List)getJdoTemplate().find(Bike.class);
    }

    public Bike getBike(String serialNo) {
        Collection c = getJdoTemplate().find(Bike.class,
            "serialNo == '" + serialNo + "'");
        Bike b = null;
        if(c.size() > 0) {
            b = (Bike)c.iterator().next();
        }
        return b;
    }

    public Bike getBike(int bikeId) {
        return (Bike)getJdoTemplate().
            getObjectById(Bike.class, new Long(bikeId));
    }

    public void saveBike(Bike bike) {
        getJdoTemplate().makePersistent(bike);
    }

    public void deleteBike(Bike bike) {
        getJdoTemplate().deletePersistent(bike);
    }

    //etc.
```

*This is not a full JDO query language query; it's simply a filter. JDO 2.0 will add a convenience query string, so that you can add a full JDO query as a single string without needing to build a full query.*

Finally, you need to set up some configuration to wire it all together. First, Example 5-12 gives the JDO configuration.

**Example 5-12.** kodo.properties

```
# To evaluate or purchase a license key, visit http://www.solarmetric.com
kodo.LicenseKey: YOUR_LICENSE_KEY_HERE

javax.jdo.PersistenceManagerFactoryClass: kodo.jdbc.runtime.
JDBCPersistenceManagerFactory
javax.jdo.option.ConnectionDriverName: com.mysql.jdbc.Driver
javax.jdo.option.ConnectionUserName: bikestore
javax.jdo.option.ConnectionPassword:
javax.jdo.option.ConnectionURL: jdbc:mysql://localhost/bikestore
javax.jdo.option.Optimistic: true
javax.jdo.option.RetainValues: true
javax.jdo.option.NontransactionalRead: true
javax.jdo.option.RestoreValues: true

kodo.Log: DefaultLevel=WARN, Runtime=INFO, Tool=INFO
kodo.PersistenceManagerImpl: DetachOnClose=true
```

The Spring context will need to wire together the JDO persistence manager, the persistence manager factory, the façade, and any services on the façade. That's done in the context (Example 5-13).

*Notice the detachOnClose. This makes sure that JDO loads anything that's lazy before the connection goes away, so that other parts of your application, like the view, can only access beans that have already been loaded.*

**Example 5-13.** RentABikeApp-servlet.xml

```xml
<bean id="jdofactory" class="org.springframework.orm.jdo.
LocalPersistenceManagerFactoryBean">
    <property name="configLocation">
        <value>E:\RentABikeApp\war\WEB-INF\kodo.properties</value>
    </property>
</bean>

<bean id="transactionManager" class="org.springframework.orm.jdo.
JdoTransactionManager">
    <property name="persistenceManagerFactory">
        <ref local="jdofactory"/>
    </property>
</bean>

<bean id="rentaBike" class="com.springbook.KodoRentABike">
    <property name="storeName"><value>Bruce's Bikes</value></property>
    <property name="persistenceManagerFactory">
        <ref local="jdofactory"/>
    </property>
</bean>
```

Recall that you've already got a test case that uses the façade, so you can build it and let it rip.

# What just happened?

This is a perfect example of the power of Spring. You've radically changed the implementation of your persistence layer, but you haven't affected the rest of the application *at all*. Here's how it works.

Spring first uses dependency injection to resolve all of the dependencies. Loading the context configures JDO with the data source that you provided, and then sets the persistence manager factory in the façade JDO implementation. Then, when you call a method on the façade, Spring gets you a persistence manager and uses it to process the query that you supply. You can look at it this way: Spring provides a generic JDO façade method, called the template. You plug in the details, and give control to Spring.

When you're biking or when you're coding, one of the most important metrics is efficiency. How much work can you do with each turn of the pedals, or each line of code? Consider the JDO version of the application. The most compelling thing about the Spring programming model is the efficiency. To see what I mean, think about what you don't see here:

- You don't have exception management cluttering the lower levels of your application. With Spring's unchecked exceptions, you can get the exception where it's appropriate to do something with it.
- You don't have resource management. Where JDBC has connections, JDO has the persistence manager. Spring configures the persistence manager factory, and manages the persistence manager within the template for you.
- You aren't forced to manage transactions and security in the façade. Spring lets you configure these things easily so that you can strip all of the ugly details out of your façade layer and let it concentrate on using the persistent model.

All of this is done for you in the Spring template, in code that comes with the Spring framework, which you can read for better understanding or debug in a pinch. In short, you can get more leverage with each line of code, much like running your bike in a higher gear. That's the bottom line for all of the most successful frameworks and programming languages.

# Using Hibernate with Spring

Hibernate has long been the persistence framework of choice for Spring developers. Although the Spring team continues to improve the integration with other persistence frameworks, Hibernate remains the most widely used persistence framework with Spring. It's fitting that these two lightweight solutions helped each other succeed. They go quite well together. In this example, we'll show how to integrate Spring and Hibernate.

Hibernate is an outstanding persistence framework. It's popular, it's relatively fast, and it's free. It has rich mapping support and a convenient usage model that's made it popular with developers across the world. Hibernate holds up very well in small- and intermediate-size projects. In fact, though it's nonstandard, you could say that behind EJB, Hibernate is the most popular persistence framework in the world.

## How do I do that?

Now that you've configured Spring with an ORM, you know the basic flow, with a persistent domain model and a façade. Since Spring ships with Hibernate dependencies, you can just copy them from Spring's /dist folder to your /lib folder: *hibernate2.jar, aopalliance.jar, cglib-full-2.0.2. jar, dom4j.jar, ehcache-1.1.jar*, and *odmg.jar*.

Since Hibernate uses reflection, there's no byte code enhancement step. All you've got to do to make the model persistent is to create the mappings, and refer to them in the context. Examples 5-14, 5-15, and 5-16 show the mappings.

**Example 5-14.** Bike.hbm.xml

```xml
<hibernate-mapping>
    <class name="com.springbook.Bike" table="bikes">
        <id name="bikeId" column="bikeid" type="java.lang.Integer"
                unsaved-value="-1">
            <generator class="native"></generator>
        </id>
        <property name="manufacturer" column="manufacturer" type="string"/>
        <property name="model" column="model" type="string"/>
        <property name="frame" column="frame" type="int"/>
        <property name="serialNo" column="serialno" type="string"/>
        <property name="weight" column="weight" type="java.lang.Double"/>
        <property name="status" column="status" type="string"/>
        <set name="reservations">
            <key column="bikeId"/>
            <one-to-many class="com.springbook.Reservation"/>
        </set>
    </class>
</hibernate-mapping>
```

*The Hibernate version of this mapping is a bit less awkward than the JDO counterpart. It has a richer identification generation library.*

**Example 5-15.** Customer.hbm.xml

```xml
<hibernate-mapping>
    <class name="com.springbook.Customer" table="customers">
        <id name="custId" column="custid" type="java.lang.Integer"
            unsaved-value="-1">
          <generator class="native"></generator>
        </id>
        <property name="firstName" column="firstname" type="string"/>
        <property name="lastName" column="lastname" type="string"/>
        <set name="reservations">
            <key column="custId"/>
            <one-to-many class="com.springbook.Reservation"/>
        </set>
    </class>
</hibernate-mapping>
```

**Example 5-16.** Reservation.hbm.xml

```xml
<hibernate-mapping>
    <class name="com.springbook.Reservation" table="reservations">
        <id name="reservationId" column="resid" type="java.lang.Integer"
            unsaved-value="-1">
          <generator class="native"></generator>
        </id>
        <property name="reservationDate" column="resdate" type="date"/>
        <many-to-one name="bike" column="bikeId" class="com.springbook.Bike"
                    cascade="none"/>
        <many-to-one name="customer" column="custId"
            class="com.springbook.Customer"
                    cascade="none"/>
    </class>
</hibernate-mapping>
```

In the context, you need to configure Hibernate properties, configure the session factory, and plug the session factory into the façade. The transaction strategies with the JDO context, the iBATIS context and the Hibernate context are the same, as they should be. That's part of what dependency injection is doing for you. Example 5-17 shows the changes to the context.

**Example 5-17.** RentABikeApp-servlet.xml

```xml
<bean name="rentaBike" class="com.springbook.HibRentABike">
    <property name="storeName"><value>Bruce's Bikes</value></property>
    <property name="sessionFactory">
        <ref local="sessionFactory"/>
    </property>
</bean>

<bean id="sessionFactory"
    class="org.springframework.orm.hibernate.LocalSessionFactoryBean">
    <property name="dataSource"><ref local="dataSource"/></property>
```

**Chapter 5: OR Persistence**

**Example 5-17.** RentABikeApp-servlet.xml (continued)

```xml
<property name="mappingResources">
    <list>
            <value>com/springbook/Bike.hbm.xml</value>
            <value>com/springbook/Customer.hbm.xml</value>
            <value>com/springbook/Reservation.hbm.xml</value>
    </list>
</property>
<property name="hibernateProperties">
    <props>
            <prop key="hibernate.dialect">
            net.sf.hibernate.dialect.MySQLDialect
            </prop>
            <prop key="hibernate.show_sql">true</prop>
    </props>
</property>
</bean>
```

Since you've already got a façade interface, you need only a Hibernate implementation. You can use templates, just as with JDO. For finders, specify a Hibernate query language (HQL) statement. For updates, all that you need to specify is the new object to be stored. Example 5-18 is the remarkably thin façade.

**Example 5-18.** HibRentABike.java

```java
package com.springbook;

import org.springframework.orm.hibernate.support.HibernateDaoSupport;

import java.util.List;
import java.util.Date;
import java.util.Set;

import net.sf.hibernate.Query;

public class HibRentABike extends HibernateDaoSupport implements RentABike {
    private String name;

    public List getBikes() {
        return getHibernateTemplate().find("from Bike");
    }

    public Bike getBike(String serialNo) {
        Bike b = null;
        List bikes = getHibernateTemplate().
            find("from Bike where serialNo = ?", serialNo);
        if(bikes.size() > 0) {
            b = (Bike)bikes.get(0);
        }
        return b;
    }
```

> Hibernate users often put all of the mapping classes into separate files, unlike JDO. You don't have to; it's just the way that Hibernate users typically prefer to manage things.

**Example 5-18.** HibRentABike.java (continued)

```java
public Bike getBike(int bikeId) {
    return (Bike)getHibernateTemplate().
        load(Bike.class, new Integer(bikeId));
}

public void saveBike(Bike bike) {
    getHibernateTemplate().saveOrUpdate(bike);
}

public void deleteBike(Bike bike) {
    getHibernateTemplate().delete(bike);
}

public void setStoreName(String name) {
    this.name = name;
}

public String getStoreName() {
    return this.name;
}

public List getCustomers() {
    return getHibernateTemplate().find("from Customer");
}

public Customer getCustomer(int custId) {
    return (Customer)getHibernateTemplate().
        load(Customer.class, new Integer(custId));
}

public List getReservations() {
    return getHibernateTemplate().find("from Reservation");
}

public List getReservations(Customer customer) {
    return getHibernateTemplate().
        find("from Reservation where custId = ?", customer.getCustId());
}

public List getReservations(Bike bike) {
    return getHibernateTemplate().
        find("from Reservation where bikeId = ?", bike.getBikeId());
}

public List getReservations(Date date) {
    return getHibernateTemplate().
        find("from Reservation where resdate = ?", date);
}

public Reservation getReservation(int resId) {
    return (Reservation)getHibernateTemplate().
```

**Example 5-18.** HibRentABike.java (continued)

```
        load(Reservation.class, new Integer(resId));
    }
}
```

# What just happened?

The Hibernate flow is pretty much the same as the JDO flow. The Spring JDO template represents a set of default DAO methods. All that you need to do is customize them, usually with a HQL query statement, and possibly the values for parameters to any HQL parameterized queries. Then Spring takes control, getting a session, firing the query, and managing any exceptions.

Once again, you see exceptional leverage. Example 5-19 gives the typical Hibernate method that you'd need to write without Spring.

**Example 5-19.** HibRentABike.java

```
public List getBikesOldWay( ) throws Exception {
        // Relies on other static code for configuration
        // and generation of SessionFactory.  Might look like:

        // Configuration config = new Configuration( );
        // config.addClass(Bike.class).addClass(Customer.class).
        //          addClass(Reservation.class);
        // SessionFactory mySessionFactory = Configuration.
        //          buildSessionFactory( );

        List bikes = null;
        Session s = null;
        try {
            s = mySessionFactory.openSession( );
            bikes = s.find("from Bike");
        }catch (Exception ex) {
            //handle exception gracefully
        }finally {
            s.close( );
        }
        return bikes;
    }
```

Example 5-20 shows, again, the Spring counterpart.

**Example 5-20.** HibRentABike.java

```
    public List getBikes( ) {
        return getHibernateTemplate( ).find("from Bike");
    }
```

Strong typing is for weak programmers. Each building block of an application should strive do one thing well, and only once.

## What about...

...alternatives to Hibernate? Hibernate is indeed free, fast, effective, and popular. It's been proven under fire, and has excellent performance and flexibility. Most tools have good Hibernate support, and Hibernate supports every database that matters. I still recommend Hibernate for small and intermediate applications.

So far, as an open source framework, the persistence community can't be quick enough to praise Hibernate or condemn the alternatives. Such blind worship leads to cultish religious decision making. There are some things that competitors do better. If your application has some of these characteristics, you might be best served to look elsewhere:

*Standards*
> JDO and JDBC solutions conform to a standard. Although it's open source code, Hibernate does not conform to a standard. You have to trust the motivations of JBoss group and the founders to do the right thing for decades, and for any framework, that's proven to be a dicey proposition so far.

*Management*
> Other solutions are easier to manage. For example, Kodo JDO and TopLink have management consoles that make it easier to manage caching scenarios, and eager or lazy-loading scenarios.

*Mapping*
> Other frameworks have more powerful and flexible mapping support. If you do not control your schema, you may be best served with another solution. Also, if you prefer to map your schema with GUI tools, then something like JDO Genie or Cayenne may work best for you.

In general, using mainstream frameworks may be the right choice in the end, but often you can find a much better fit with a little digging. Hibernate certainly deserves consideration, but there are other good choices out there, too.

## Running a Test Case

The test case is easy to run. You've already got it. It's the one that you ran with the façade.

## How do I do that?

Since the test case exists, you can run the existing façade test. You'll just have to make sure that you set up your test data correctly, and you can use the application context unchanged. That's the power, and testability, of Spring.

## What just happened?

You used the existing test case. That's nice, because you only need to manage the incremental details for the database. In the next chapter, you'll start to dig into services that you can add to your application with Spring's AOP.

# CHAPTER 6

# Services and AOP

Most kayakers that I know are demented and proud of it. We tend to look for those places on a river that are dangerous enough to scare but tame enough to play. While I was learning to surf hydraulics on Barton Creek at high water, I slipped into a hydraulic to play, but couldn't get out. I flipped, upstream, and the hydraulic quickly flipped me 360 degrees, so that I was upright again. I frantically surfed a little while longer, then flipped again, and then all of my control deserted me. The hydraulic then took over, and spun me around like a window shade. When my friends laughed and grabbed their cameras instead of their safety ropes, I bailed, coughing and gagging my way to the bank to nurse my battered ego. I mumbled something about my boat being the source of the problem. Predictably, one of my friends got into my boat, and then toyed with my nemesis, the killer hydraulic, for a while. To make things worse, he then threw his paddle onto the bank, and played some more. He said, "Bruce, it's not the boat. It's how you use it." I'm still fuming today.

I'm starting to recognize that the same is true of many Java services. It's not the service; it's how you apply it. You can get a whole lot more leverage out of certain services like transactions, security, and logging by packaging them and using them in a way that simplifies them and eliminates duplication in the rest of the code. Spring uses aspect-oriented programming (AOP) to manage these services, called *crosscutting concerns*. In this chapter, you'll learn to build and configure such a service using an *interceptor*.

## Building a Service

The core functions of your application are roughly complete, but it's going to be hard to trace what changes a user made, and when. In this example, you'll build an audit trail that records a log record whenever someone takes an action that changes the database. Rather than add the same code in many different places, you'll build a simple Spring service to do the job. You'll focus on the Hibernate implementation that you built earlier.

Object-oriented languages handle some problems pretty well, but they don't handle crosscutting concerns, common in enterprise developments, very well. Figure 6-1 shows a method with some common enterprise services that crosscut many methods in DAO and façade layers.

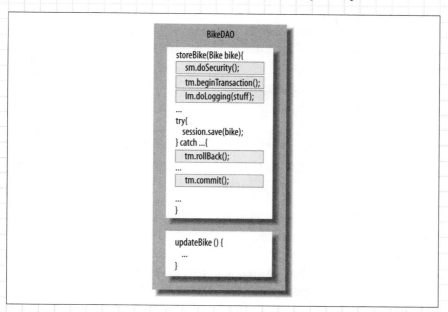

**Figure 6-1.** Some classic enterprise crosscutting concerns

To handle crosscutting concerns, you might decide to use a container. Most containers accept only components that match their specification, and provide services to components once they're in the container. Heavyweight container architectures, like EJB 1.x and 2.x, handle crosscutting concerns, but they force you to write code that depends on your given container. You can't take the code out of the container and expect it to run, and since the container takes too long to start, the result is difficult to test.

Lightweight containers that use AOP technologies accept components too, but the component is a simple POJO. You can then use AOP to attach services to the POJO. We'll get into how this works later in the chapter, but for now, think of this feature as the ability to add declarative services to POJO. In Spring, you implement declarative services with configuration rather than code, so you can change services on the fly through changes in the context.

## How do I do that?

The interceptor strategy uses three objects: the target (our façade), a proxy object that Spring creates for you, and an interceptor, which you'll build. Essentially, the proxy imitates the target—wherever you would use an instance of the target object, Spring will use the proxy instead. The proxy will pass all calls to the object through a series of interceptors that you'll configure in the context. Depending on the type of interceptors, the call might pass through the interceptor before reaching the target, on the way back from the target, or both.

You've got to do three things:

1. Create your service, which we'll call an interceptor. Another word for interceptors is *advice*.

2. Configure the beans: the interceptor and the target object.

3. Configure the proxy—identify the proxy, the target object, and the methods that will use our service.

To build advice, you'll simply implement an interface. Think of advice as something that will happen at some event in a program's execution. Spring has four types of advice:

*Before advice*
Spring fires this type of advice before it invokes a method that you specify, called the target method. This type of advice implements the MethodBeforeAdvice interface.

*After Returning advice*
Spring fires this type of advice after returning from your target method. After Returning advice implements the AfterReturningAdvice interface.

*Throws advice*
Spring fires this type of advice when your target method throws an exception. This type of advice implements the ThrowsAdvice interface.

*Around advice*
Spring fires this type of advice before a method, and allows you to choose whether to invoke the target method. After the target method returns, you can add additional code. This is also called an interceptor.

In general, you should use the simplest type of advice that will solve your problem. For this example, you'll use before advice, and you'll build on the Hibernate interface. The interceptor will implement the Method-BeforeAdvice interface. It will do the logging. Don't worry about how it gets invoked just yet. Example 6-1 gives the advice.

**Example 6-1.** LoggingBefore.java

```java
public class LoggingBefore implements MethodBeforeAdvice {

    private SessionFactory factory;

    public SessionFactory getFactory() {
        return factory;
    }

    public void setFactory(SessionFactory factory) {
        this.factory = factory;
    }

    public void before(Method method, Object[] objects, Object o)
            throws Throwable {

        Session s = null;
        LogEvent le = new LogEvent(method.getName(), new Date());
        try {
            s = factory.openSession();
            s.save(le);
        } catch (Exception ex) {
            //log the exception
        } finally {
            s.close();
        }
    }
}
```

*This session factory is the resource that lets you access the database through Hibernate. It will be set through dependency injection.*

*This is the method that gets fired for the advice.*

The logger uses a new persistent class called *LogEvent*, whose class file and mapping file are shown in Example 6-2 and Example 6-3.

**Example 6-2.** LogEvent.java

```java
package com.springbook;
import java.util.Date;

public class LogEvent {
    private int eventId;
    private String methodName;
    private Date dateTime;
    private String message;

    public LogEvent() {}

    public LogEvent(String methodName, Date date, String message) {
        this.eventId = -1;
        this.methodName = methodName;
```

**Example 6-2.** LogEvent.java

```java
            this.dateTime = date;
            this.message = message;
    }

    public LogEvent(String methodName, Date date) { this(methodName, date, "");
}
    public String getMessage() { return message; }

    public void setMessage(String message) { this.message = message;}

    public int getEventId() { return eventId;}

    public void setEventId(int eventId) { this.eventId = eventId;}

    public String getMethodName() {return methodName; }

    public void setMethodName(String methodName) { this.methodName = methodName; }

    public Date getDateTime() { return dateTime; }

    public void setDateTime(Date dateTime) { this.dateTime = dateTime; }
}
```

**Example 6-3.** LogEvent.hbm.xml

```xml
<?xml version="1.0"?>
<!DOCTYPE hibernate-mapping PUBLIC
"-//Hibernate/Hibernate Mapping DTD//EN"
"http://hibernate.sf.net/hibernate-mapping-2.0.dtd">
<hibernate-mapping>
    <class name="com.springbook.LogEvent" table="eventlog">
        <id name="eventId" column="eventId" type="java.lang.Integer"
            unsaved-value="-1">
            <generator class="native"></generator>
        </id>
        <property name="methodName" column="methodname" type="string"/>
        <property name="dateTime" column="datetime" type="date"/>
        <property name="message" column="message" type="string"/>
    </class>
</hibernate-mapping>
```

For now, you can manually invoke it in a test case. In this case, you can simply count the number of events that exist in the database prior to running the advice, then compare that to the number of events in the database after running it. For the test in Example 6-4, it doesn't matter which method is being logged, just that the logger is activated.

**Example 6-4.** ControllerTest.java

```java
public void testLocal() throws Exception {
    LoggingBefore lb = new LoggingBefore();
    SessionFactory factory =
            (SessionFactory)ctx.getBean("sessionFactory");

    // getCurEventsCount() is a private utility method that
    // gets the current number of log events in the database
    int initialCount = getCurEventsCount();

    lb.setFactory(factory);
    try {
        lb.before((Method)this.getClass().getMethods()[0], null, null);
    } catch (Throwable t) {
        fail(t.getMessage());
    }

    int afterCount = getCurEventsCount();
    assertEquals("Should add one event to log",
            initialCount, afterCount - 1);
}
```

## What just happened?

You've just built a service. Unlike other container architectures, Spring does not define the complete package of services that components in the container can use. The services are ideal for our purposes:

- The clean programming model defines exactly how a service must be packaged.
- The services strategy is minimal, requiring very little of the service builder.
- The services are easy to test, since they can run outside of the container.
- The services can be used elsewhere; they are compatible with a standard called the Aspect Alliance.

Of course, right now, the service doesn't do anything. You need to attach it to something real.

# Configuring a Service

You've built an audit service that will help you keep track of changes in the application. Now, you need to attach the service to your code. You'll configure the service in this lab.

# How do I do that?

The interceptor strategy uses three objects: the target (our façade), a proxy object that Spring creates for you, and an interceptor, which you'll build. Recall that you've got to do three things:

1. Configure the advice.
2. Configure the advisor, including a target object, target methods, and the advice.
3. Configure the target object.
4. Configure the proxy to use the advisor.

The target object already exists: our façade. The proxy already exists, because you used it for transactions. You need to configure the advice and add it to your proxy. Example 6-5 shows the changes to the context.

**Example 6-5.** RentABikeApp-servlet.xml

```
<beans>
    <bean id="transactionManager"
    class="org.springframework.orm.hibernate.HibernateTransactionManager">
        <property name="sessionFactory">
            <ref local="sessionFactory"/>
        </property>
    </bean>

    <bean id="transactionInterceptor"
class="org.springframework.transaction.interceptor.TransactionInterceptor">
        <property name="transactionManager">
            <ref local="transactionManager"/>
        </property>
        <property name="transactionAttributeSource">
            <value>
                com.springbook.HibernateRentABike.save*=PROPAGATION_REQUIRED
            </value>
        </property>
    </bean>

    <bean id="loggingBeforeInterceptor"
        class="com.springbook.interceptors.LoggingBefore">
        <property name="factory">
            <ref local="sessionFactory"/>
        </property>
    </bean>

    <bean id="rentaBikeTarget" class="com.springbook.HibRentABike">
        <property name="storeName">
            <value>Bruce's Bikes</value>
        </property>
        <property name="sessionFactory">
            <ref local="sessionFactory"/>
```

*These are the changes to the context. You see the proxy (rentaBike), the target (rentaBike-Target), and the interceptor (rentaBike-Interceptor) all defined here.*

**Example 6-5.** RentABikeApp-servlet.xml (continued)

```
        </property>
    </bean>

    <bean id="rentaBike"
        class="org.springframework.aop.framework.ProxyFactoryBean">
        <property name="proxyInterfaces">
            <value>com.springbook.RentABike</value>
        </property>
        <property name="interceptorNames">
            <list>
                <value>loggingBeforeInterceptor</value>
                <value>transactionInterceptor</value>
                <value>rentaBikeTarget</value>
            </list>
        </property>
    </bean>

    <!-- etc. -->

    <bean id="dataSource" class="org.springframework.jdbc.datasource.
DriverManagerDataSource">
        <property name="driverClassName">
            <value>com.mysql.jdbc.Driver</value>
        </property>
        <property name="url">
            <value>jdbc:mysql://localhost/bikestore</value>
        </property>
        <property name="username"><value>bikestore</value></property>
    </bean>
</beans>
```

Now, you can let it rip. Notice that you get an audit trail whenever you change any record.

## What just happened?

So far, most Java developers use programmatic services—you load them and access them explicitly. Spring also allows declarative services—you specify them in configuration rather than code—with proxy objects. A proxy object stands in for a target object, forwarding calls to the target after providing its service. The proxy and its target have the same interface. CORBA used proxies to do distributed communication, without forcing us to create any code for distribution: the intelligence was in the proxy. With AOP, the job of the proxy is to apply advice to remote objects.

Our example uses simple *before advice*. Now, let's look at *around advice*, the most complex model. If you understand the most advanced flow, the others should be easy. Figure 6-2 shows how advice works in Spring.

The BikeDAO is the target object. It has the business code. To configure an interceptor, you specify a proxy. The proxy maintains a chain of interceptors. An object calls a method on the proxy instead of the target object. When you call a method on the proxy or fire an exception, the proxy calls the first interceptor in the chain. Each interceptor does its work and then invokes the next interceptor in the chain. The last interceptor invokes the target method or exception. After the target does its work, the interceptors just return right back down the chain.

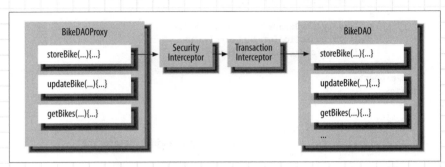

**Figure 6-2.** Spring attaches services to POJOs through proxies that call an interceptor chain

In this example, you configured a proxy on a target object. You told the proxy to apply your interceptor to any method in the target, but you could have just as easily specified a subset of the methods with a regular expression. Example 6-6 is the same advice, coded as an interceptor.

**Example 6-6.** LoggingAround.java

```java
public class LoggingAround implements MethodInterceptor {
    private SessionFactory factory;

    public SessionFactory getFactory() {
        return factory;
    }

    public void setFactory(SessionFactory factory) {
        this.factory = factory;
    }

    private void logEvent(String methodName, String message)
            throws Exception {

        Session s = null;
        LogEvent le = new LogEvent(methodName, new Date( ), message);
        try {
            s = factory.openSession( );
            s.save(le);
```

**Example 6-6.** LoggingAround.java (continued)

```java
        } catch (Exception ex) {
            //log the exception
        } finally {
            s.close();
        }
    }

    public Object invoke(MethodInvocation methodInvocation)
            throws Throwable {
        logEvent(methodInvocation.getMethod().getName(), "Entering call.");
        Object result = methodInvocation.proceed();
        logEvent(methodInvocation.getMethod().getName(), "Leaving call.");
        return result;
    }
}
```

Example 6-7 shows the new configuration.

**Example 6-7.** RentABikeApp-servlet.xml

```xml
<bean id="loggingAround" class="com.springbook.interceptors.LoggingAround">
    <property name="factory"><ref local="sessionFactory"/></property>
</bean>

<bean id="saveAdvisor" class="org.springframework.aop.support.
RegexpMethodPointcutAdvisor">
    <property name="advice">
        <ref local="loggingAround"/>
    </property>
    <property name="patterns">
        <list>
            <value>.*save.*</value>
        </list>
    </property>
</bean>

<bean id="rentaBikeTarget" class="com.springbook.HibRentABike">
    <property name="storeName"><value>Bruce's Bikes</value></property>
    <property name="sessionFactory"><ref local="sessionFactory"/></property>
</bean>

<bean id="rentaBike"
    class="org.springframework.aop.framework.ProxyFactoryBean">
    <property name="proxyInterfaces">
        <value>com.springbook.RentABike</value>
    </property>
    <property name="interceptorNames">
        <list>
            <value>transactionInterceptor</value>
            <value>saveAdvisor</value>
            <value>rentaBikeTarget</value>
        </list>
```

**Example 6-7.** RentABikeApp-servlet.xml (continued)

```
    </property>
</bean>
```

The table results in Example 6-8 show the before and after advice being called only for save-related methods.

**Example 6-8.** Examining the contents of the logging table

```
+----------+--------------+------------+-----------------+
| eventId  | methodName   | dateTime   | message         |
+----------+--------------+------------+-----------------+
|       14 | saveBike     | 2004-10-13 | Entering call.  |
|       15 | saveBike     | 2004-10-13 | Leaving call.   |
|       16 | saveCustomer | 2004-10-13 | Entering call.  |
|       17 | saveCustomer | 2004-10-13 | Leaving call.   |
|       18 | saveBike     | 2004-10-13 | Entering call.  |
|       19 | saveBike     | 2004-10-13 | Leaving call.   |
+----------+--------------+------------+-----------------+
```

The end result is exactly what we expect. Each time one of the specified methods gets called on our target, the advice fires. We've got declarative auditing. In fact, we can code any service and make it declarative.

# Using an Autoproxy

So far, you've explicitly and manually created each proxy. Spring also has the ability to automatically create a proxy, or *autoproxy*. The goal of the autoproxy is to apply the same signature to a number of methods. In this lab, you'll use an autoproxy to attach profiling code to all of the classes in the application.

## How do I do that?

Spring 1.1 lets you do autoproxying in two ways. You can:

- Specify a configuration and apply it to named beans context.
- Use source-level metadata (added to the JDK in Java 5, but available through Apache Commons annotations today).

In this example, you're going to be proxying named beans. As before, you'll first need some advice. Example 6-9 shows around advice that prints profiling statements before and after Spring enters a method.

**Example 6-9.** ProfilingInterceptory.java

```java
public class ProfilingInterceptor implements MethodInterceptor{
    public Object invoke(MethodInvocation methodInvocation)
```

**Example 6-9.** ProfilingInterceptory.java (continued)

```
            throws Throwable {
        long start = System.currentTimeMillis( );
        Object results = methodInvocation.proceed( );
        long end = System.currentTimeMillis( );
        System.out.println("Method: " +
            methodInvocation.getMethod().getName( ) + " took " +
            (end - start) + " ms.");
        return results;
    }
}
```

Next, configure it. Don't specify a single target, but a regular expression. Spring will apply the advice to all of the beans that match. Specify the autoproxy, the advice, and the targets (Example 6-10).

**Example 6-10.** RentABikeApp-servlet.xml

```
<bean name="profilerAround"
    class="com.springbook.interceptors.ProfilingInterceptor"/>

<bean name="profilingAutoProxy" class="org.springframework.aop.framework.
autoproxy.BeanNameAutoProxyCreator">

    <property name="beanNames"><value>rentaBike*</value></property>
    <property name="interceptorNames">
        <list>
            <value>profilerAround</value>
        </list>
    </property>
</bean>
```

Now, when you run the application on *std.out* console, you can see that the application tells you when it enters or leaves a given method and how much time the method took to execute (Example 6-11).

**Example 6-11.** Standard out from running application

```
Entered toString
Method: toString took 0 ms.
Entered isSingleton
Method: isSingleton took 0 ms.
Entered getObject
Method: getObject took 0 ms.
Entered getObject
Method: getObject took 0 ms.
Entered getObject
Method: getObject took 0 ms.
Entered getObject
Method: getObject took 0 ms.
Entered getObject
Method: getObject took 0 ms.
```

**Example 6-11.** *Standard out from running application (continued)*

```
Entered getObject
Method: getObject took 0 ms.
Entered saveBike
Method: saveBike took 31 ms.
Entered getBike
Method: getBike took 78 ms.
Entered deleteBike
Method: deleteBike took 62 ms.
Entered getBikes
Method: getBikes took 47 ms.
```

## What just happened?

This example has two major differences from the previous one: we're working on multiple beans, and we're using a different type of advice. Let's take a closer look.

Drill down on the interceptor itself first. You'll notice that the MethodInterceptor advice, inside the invoke method, does some work, calls proceed, and then does more work. Drill down to the call to proceed in our interceptor. That method calls the next interceptor in the chain, or the target method if it's at the last interceptor in the chain. You have a whole lot of flexibility here:

- You can do some work before the proceed( ), like our caching of the start time of the method. That code will execute before the target method.

- You can do some work after the proceed( ), but before the return. That code will execute after the target method.

- You can decide not to call proceed( ). In this case, the target method will not execute.

- Your code can fire an exception, changing the flow of control. In your exception, you may or may not decide to call proceed( ).

Otherwise, this kind of advice works just like the others. So which kind of advice should you use? Spring founder Rod Johnson suggests that you use the weakest type of advice that will work for you.

There's another difference between this example and the last: the target. You're proxying multiple targets. After Spring loads a context, it takes a post-processing pass through the beans of the context. In this pass, Spring applies this proxy definition to all of the beans in the context. It first decides if the bean matches the specified target. If it does, it creates the specified proxy.

# Advising Exceptions

Often, you'll want to attach a service to exception logic, rather than mainstream code. It's especially important when exceptions force a major change in application flow, such as rolling back when an exception occurs, or automatically notifying administrators when some resource runs low.

Your application schedules bikes for a small store. You can use Spring's exceptions to generate a message whenever something goes wrong in the application. For simplicity, you'll send it to the console for now.

## How do I do that?

The first job is to build an advisor. Use a simple class that implements the ThrowsAdvice interface, like in Example 6-12.

**Example 6-12.** ExceptionInterceptor.java

```java
public class ExceptionInterceptor implements ThrowsAdvice {
    public void afterThrowing(Method m, Object[] args,
            Object target, Exception ex) {

        System.out.println("Call to method " + m.getName() +
            " on class " + target.getClass().getName() +
            " resulted in exception of type " + ex.getClass().getName());
        System.out.println("Exception message: " + ex.getMessage());
    }
}
```

Keep in mind that the ThrowsAdvice interface contains no method signatures; you can implement as many versions of afterThrowing as you want. Each *must* declare that last parameter as a subclass of Throwable. The other three parameters are optional.

Configure the parameters for the advice interceptor in the context. Next, you'll configure the advice (note that Example 6-13 goes back to using the ProxyFactoryBean from the first part of this chapter, as opposed to an autoproxy, like the previous example).

*This is the target.*

**Example 6-13.** RentABikeApp-servlet.xml

*This is the interceptor.*

```xml
<bean id="exceptionInterceptor"
    class="com.springbook.interceptors.ExceptionInterceptor"/>
<bean id="rentaBike"
    class="org.springframework.aop.framework.ProxyFactoryBean">

    <property name="proxyInterfaces">
        <value>com.springbook.RentABike</value>
```

**Example 6-13.** RentABikeApp-servlet.xml (continued)

```
    </property>
    <property name="interceptorNames">
        <list>
            <value>exceptionInterceptor</value>
            <value>transactionInterceptor</value>
            <value>saveAdvisor</value>
            <value>rentaBikeTarget</value>
        </list>
    </property>
</bean>
```

In this case, notice that we're still targeting methods. You'll get notified whenever a serious exception occurs. To make sure it's working, let's try to remove a bike that doesn't exist (Example 6-14).

**Example 6-14.** ControllerTest.java

```
public void testRemoveNonExistentBike() throws Exception {
    Bike b = new Bike(99, "me", "mine", 1, "1", 12.00, "good");
    store.deleteBike(b);
}
```

The console output in Example 6-15 is the result.

**Example 6-15.** Standard output from running application

```
Call to method deleteBike on class $Proxy0 resulted in exception of type org.
springframework.orm.hibernate.HibernateSystemException

Exception message: Batch update row count wrong: 0; nested exception is net.sf.
hibernate.HibernateException: Batch update row count wrong: 0
```

## What just happened?

There's no magic here. Spring uses the same mechanism, proxies, to intercept exception logic. We told the proxy to attach our interceptor to all of the methods that updated the database. Within our exception logic, we can decide what to do. In our case, we looked at the exception and decided which exceptions were important to us. We then simply dumped some information to the console, and returned control where it belonged: in this case, the façade method.

## Testing a Service with Mocks

Testing AOP applications seems difficult, but we'll give you a couple of techniques that simplify it. In this example, you'll learn how to use mock objects with aspects.

# Why do I care?

When you use an aspect, it's often difficult to know if that aspect is working correctly. Since it's not main-line code, the testing strategy is not always clear. By mocking your aspect, you can confirm that it's fired when you expect it to be.

# How do I do that?

We're going to create a test case, and call a target method within the test case (Examples 6-16 and 6-17).

**Example 6-16.** InterceptMe.java

```
// simple intercept to proxy
public interface InterceptMe {
    void interceptThisMethod();
}
```

**Example 6-17.** MockInterceptorTest.java

```
public class MockInterceptorTest extends TestCase implements InterceptMe {
    public void interceptThisMethod() {
        // empty method
    }
}
```

Then, in our actual test method, we'll configure a proxy for the test case, and configure the proxy to intercept all the methods in our test interface (Example 6-18).

**Example 6-18.** MockInterceptorTest.java

```
public void testLoggingInterceptor() throws Exception {
    Advice advice = new LoggingAround();
    ProxyFactory proxyFactory = new ProxyFactory(this);
    proxyFactory.addAdvice(advice);
    InterceptMe target = (InterceptMe)proxyFactory.getProxy();
    target.interceptThisMethod();
}
```

Finally, we'll use a mock object to record our expected behavior, and verify the behavior when we're done. In this case, remember the definition of the LoggingAround interceptor (Example 6-19).

**Example 6-19.** LoggingAround.java

```
public class LoggingAround implements MethodInterceptor {
    private SessionFactory factory;
```

**Example 6-19.** LoggingAround.java (continued)

```java
    public SessionFactory getFactory() {
        return factory;
    }

    public void setFactory(SessionFactory factory) {
        this.factory = factory;
    }

    private void logEvent(String methodName, String message)
            throws Exception {
        Session s = null;
        LogEvent le = new LogEvent(methodName, new Date(), message);
        try {
            s = factory.openSession();
            s.save(le);
        } catch (Exception ex) {
            //log the exception
        } finally {
            s.close();
        }
    }

    public Object invoke(MethodInvocation methodInvocation)
            throws Throwable {
        logEvent(methodInvocation.getMethod().getName(), "Entering call.");
        Object result = methodInvocation.proceed();
        logEvent(methodInvocation.getMethod().getName(), "Leaving call.");
        return result;
    }
}
```

We're interested in verifying that it executes without actually having it write to the database. So we are going to provide a mock SessionFactory to mimic the behavior of Hibernate within the interceptor. Example 6-20 is the full test method with the mock objects added (note the programming injection of the mock SessionFactory into the interceptor).

**Example 6-20.** MockInterceptorTest.java

```java
public void testLoggingInterceptor() throws Exception {
    MockControl factoryControl =
        MockControl.createControl(SessionFactory.class);
    MockControl sessionControl =
        MockControl.createControl(Session.class);
```

**Example 6-20.** MockInterceptorTest.java (continued)

```
    SessionFactory mockFactory =
        (SessionFactory)factoryControl.getMock( );
    Session mockSession = (Session)sessionControl.getMock( );

    // this sequence will execute once before the target method...
    mockFactory.openSession( );
    factoryControl.setReturnValue(mockSession);
    mockSession.save(new LogEvent( ));
    sessionControl.setMatcher(MockControl.ALWAYS_MATCHER);
    sessionControl.setReturnValue(null);
    mockSession.close( );
    sessionControl.setReturnValue(null);

    // and once after
    mockFactory.openSession( );
    factoryControl.setReturnValue(mockSession);
    mockSession.save(new LogEvent( ));
    sessionControl.setReturnValue(null);
    mockSession.close( );
    sessionControl.setReturnValue(null);

    factoryControl.replay( );
    sessionControl.replay( );

    Advice advice = new LoggingAround( );
    ((LoggingAround)advice).setFactory(mockFactory);
    ProxyFactory proxyFactory = new ProxyFactory(this);
    proxyFactory.addAdvice(advice);
    InterceptMe target = (InterceptMe)proxyFactory.getProxy( );
    target.interceptThisMethod( );

    factoryControl.verify( );
    sessionControl.verify( );
}
```

# What just happened?

When you think about it, our interceptors are just objects. We can mock APIs in them as easily as any other service. The trick is to take advantage of Spring's light weight, and run the container in the test case. We just advised our test case.

Here, we're just trying to make sure that the service works. We're not trying to test any of the façade methods, only the advice. We attached our new service to our test case method. When the test case called the method, the advice fired, and we verified that in the mock object.

# Testing a Service with Side Effects

Of course, you didn't learn anything about the way our code used the services. To test the services, you'll need to attach them to real code and exercise the code. In your test, you can merely look for a side effect.

When you use AOP, the business objects don't always get exercised with basic out-of-container tests. You've got to run some tests in the container to make sure that transactions get committed or rolled back as they should, and that the security is behaving appropriately. Remember, *the context is part of the program!*

## How do I do that?

You'll simply exercise some code that's using an AOP service and you'll look for a known side-effect. Example 6-21 is a test case that causes an exception in the façade. We assert that the changes did not get committed.

**Example 6-21.** ControllerTest.java

```
public void testAddBadBike( ) throws Exception {
      int origCount = store.getBikes().size( );
      // collision on uniquely indexed serial number 11111
      Bike bike = new Bike(-1, "MyMan", "MyBike",
          12, "11111", 12.00, "New");
      try {
          store.saveBike(bike);
      } catch (Exception ex) {
          assertEquals(origCount, store.getBikes().size( ));
          return;
      }
      fail("Should have errored out on bad insert.");
}
```

## What just happened?

You once again fired a test case from within the container. The test case called our façade directly. The façade did a database insert, but the bad data forced the transaction to roll back. Your test case made sure that the data did not get committed by doing a second read. In the next chapter, you'll release the full power of AOP using some of Spring's pre-built interceptors.

If you've never seen AOP or interceptors before, this chapter might have been challenging for you. If you want to learn more about aspect-oriented programming or design patterns for proxying interfaces, turn to these resources:

- *AspectJ in Action*, by Ramnivas Laddad (Manning)
- *Mastering AspectJ: Aspect-Oriented Programming in Java*, by Joseph D. Gradecki and Nicholas Lesiecki (Wiley)
- "Take control with the Proxy design pattern," by David Geary (*http://www.javaworld.com/javaworld/jw-02-2002/jw-0222-designpatterns.html*)

# Transactions and Security

In mountain biking and kayaking, the most thrilling moves are running ledges. It doesn't start that way in either sport. With kayaks, you tend to do a whole lot of work to set yourself up for a few seconds of freefall. You line up against a landmark, stroke hard to build speed, push your body forward, and then simultaneously thrust with your hips and paddle off of the edge, which launches you. With bikes, you tend to pick a line through that won't smash your chain ring, line your bike up, balance yourself behind the saddle so you don't fly over the handlebars, roll forward slowly, compress your shocks, jump up to lighten the bike, and hope for the best while you're falling.

If you crash, you wonder what went wrong in freefall, but the freefall is just the result of a whole lot of setup work. With all of those steps, there's a whole lot that can go wrong. In both sports, you learn to economize your movements, and group all of the early and late motions into a forward thrust and freefall. You still have to do all of the same work, but you're able to group all of those related motions into a single package that floats in your subconscious, and doesn't take active thought. Now, I rarely crash on a drop. The freefall becomes the easy part, and pure enjoyment.

Programming is similar. If each method is a drop, then a whole lot of effort goes into cleaning up the logic that goes immediately before and after the freefall, or the main-line logic.

## Programmatic Transactions

Like most other services in Spring, you can use transactions programmatically or declaratively. When you're using a new service, it often makes sense to understand that service programmatically within a method before you break it out as a declarative service.

Sometimes, you want to hide services, and Spring certainly makes it easy to do so. Other times, you want to be explicit, such as when transactional logic is the central job of your method. Spring makes it easy to do transaction logic programmatically.

## How do I do that?

You'll use the same mechanism for transactions as you do for JDBC: templates. For programmatic transactions, you'll use a TransactionTemplate. You'll put all of the code in the transaction body that you want to execute together.

In this case, imagine that a customer wants to cancel her current reservation and make a new one for later in the week. If the new reservation fails for any reason, she wants to keep her old one. You'll add a method to RentABike called transferReservation. It will delete an existing reservation and create a new one (Example 7-1).

**Example 7-1.** HibRentABike.java

```
public void transferReservation(final Reservation oldRes,
    final Reservation newRes) throws ReservationTransferException {

    TransactionTemplate template =
        new TransactionTemplate(this.transactionManager);
        template.setPropagationBehavior(
        TransactionDefinition.PROPAGATION_REQUIRED);

        try {
    template.execute(new TransactionCallbackWithoutResult() {
            protected void doInTransactionWithoutResult(
            TransactionStatus transactionStatus) {

            getHibernateTemplate().save(newRes);
            getHibernateTemplate().delete(oldRes);
            }
        });
    } catch (Exception ex) {
        throw new ReservationTransferException();
    }
}
```

*Think of a transaction template as a generic method that manages a transaction.*

*Do this work in the transaction.*

You'll need to set up the transaction strategy for the template in the context, and create the accounts and the RentABike (Example 7-2).

**Example 7-2.** RentABike-servlet.xml

```xml
<beans>
    <bean id="sessionFactory" class="org.springframework.orm.hibernate.
LocalSessionFactoryBean">
        <property name="dataSource"><ref local="dataSource"/></property>
            <property name="mappingResources">
             <list>
                    <value>com/springbook/Bike.hbm.xml</value>
                    <value>com/springbook/Customer.hbm.xml</value>
                    <value>com/springbook/Reservation.hbm.xml</value>
                    <value>com/springbook/LogEvent.hbm.xml</value>
             </list>
            </property>
        <property name="hibernateProperties">
                <props>
                        <prop key="hibernate.dialect">
                    net.sf.hibernate.dialect.MySQLDialect
                        </prop>
                        <prop key="hibernate.show_sql">false</prop>
                </props>
        </property>
    </bean>

    <bean id="transactionManager" class="org.springframework.orm.hibernate.
HibernateTransactionManager">
        <property name="sessionFactory">
            <ref local="sessionFactory"/>
        </property>
    </bean>

    <bean id="rentaBike" class="com.springbook.HibRentABike">
            <property name="storeName">
            <value>Bruce's Bikes</value>
            </property>
            <property name="sessionFactory">
            <ref local="sessionFactory"/>
            </property>
            <property name="transactionManager">
            <ref local="transactionManager"/>
            </property>
    </bean>

    <bean id="dataSource" class="org.springframework.jdbc.datasource.
DriverManagerDataSource">
            <property name="driverClassName">
            <value>com.mysql.jdbc.Driver</value>
            </property>
            <property name="url">
            <value>jdbc:mysql://localhost/rentabike</value>
            </property>
            <property name="username"><value>bikestore</value></property>
```

*This bean sets up the transaction strategy. Here, you want to use the transaction manager that comes with Hibernate.*

**Example 7-2.** RentABike-servlet.xml (continued)

```
    </bean>
</beans>
```

*ACID stands for atomic, consistent, isolated and durable. All transactions need these properties.*

Take special care. Because you are using MySQL as the database for this example, you'll need one final step to get it to work. In order to support transactions, you have to mark your tables in MySQL as InnoDB type, which lets MySQL be transactional, with full ACID semantics.

## What just happened?

A template is a simple, default transaction-handling method. All of the boilerplate code is in the template. You just have to implement the method that does all of the work. It will either all succeed or roll back.

You're looking for two things: a pluggable architecture, and leverage. Of course, Hibernate transactions need only a command or two. Think about a native implementation. If you wanted to replace the Hibernate transactions with JTA transactions (to coordinate with changes in another database), you'd have to replace your implementation throughout your code, and you'd have to do much more work.

With your Spring implementation, you need only change configuration. The template gives you exactly what you want: a place to specify what needs to happen together successfully for the transaction to succeed.

# Configuring Simple Transactions

Now, you'll see the most useful type of transaction support: *declarative transactions*. It's time to go back and explain the configuration of the transactions on your façade. In Chapter 4, you configured the transactions without explanation. It's time to go back and fill in the holes.

Declarative transactions are perhaps the most important feature of EJB session beans. Many developers decide not to use EJB at all when they discover that you can in fact use declarative transactions without sacrificing your first-born child.

You will implement declarative transactions without ever touching the code. You only need to change the context. Just like the examples in the previous chapter, you will configure an interceptor. The interceptor defines the methods to be marked as transactional and defines their expected behavior. Some of the methods will use full transaction propagation, and some will use a lighter-weight, read-only propagation (Example 7-3).

**Example 7-3.** RentABike-servlet.xml

```xml
<bean name="transactionInterceptor" class="org.springframework.transaction.
interceptor.TransactionInterceptor">
        <property name="transactionManager">
            <ref local="transactionManager"/>
        </property>
        <property name="transactionAttributeSource">
            <value>
            com.springbook.RentABike.transferReservation=
            PROPAGATION_REQUIRED,-ReservationTransferException
            com.springbook.RentABike.save*=PROPAGATION_REQUIRED
            com.springbook.RentABike.*=PROPAGATION_REQUIRED,readOnly

            </value>
        </property>
</bean>
```

*This value marks the methods that need to be transactional. You can specify a single method, or a regular expression.*

In the definition of the behavior for the `transferReservation` method, notice that you pass the required transaction flag and the name of a checked exception. This tells your interceptor to roll back the transaction if an exception of that type is thrown; otherwise, not.

Next, you'll build a proxy that specifies the target bean, like in Example 7-4.

*Think of this bean as the behavior in the original target, plus all of the aspects that you've added. In this case, the rentaBike is a transactional version of the target.*

**Example 7-4.** RentABike-servlet.xml

```xml
<bean id="rentaBike" class="org.springframework.aop.framework.ProxyFactoryBean">
        <property name="proxyInterfaces">
          <value>com.springbook.RentABike</value>
        </property>
        <property name="interceptorNames">
            <value>transactionInterceptor,rentaBikeTarget</value>
        </property>
</bean>
```

The execution remains unchanged.

## What just happened?

You just configured declarative transactions on a POJO. When any of the methods that we specified starts, the transaction advisor will tell the underlying transaction strategy to start the transaction. When the method successfully completes, the advisor will commit the transaction. If there's an exception, the advisor will roll back. That's exactly the behavior that you're looking for.

# What about...

Java Transaction API, or JTA? So far, you've used lightweight transactions. The nice thing about Spring is that you can change the transaction strategy without rewriting any code. Spring fully supports JTA, so you can use it to span multiple databases or perform distributed transactions (called XA transactions).

XA transactions may be more powerful than the alternatives, but you don't always need them. In fact, there are at least two good reasons to use something else:

- You may need individual features in a more direct transactional API, such as the isolation level support from JDBC transactions. In that case, XA transactions won't work, because they don't provide domain-specific abstractions.
- You might need better performance. If XA transactions are overkill (such as applications that only access a single database), then XA transactions are likely to be much slower than an alternative, such as `HibernateTransactions`.

JTA tends to be the best fit when you're using multiple resources. If your application needs to commit data from the same transaction across multiple databases, then JTA will likely be your best fit.

# Transactions on Multiple Databases

If you have to refactor a simple application to use multiple resources, Spring's pluggable transaction strategies can save you a whole lot of effort. In this example, you're going to use JTA transactions to span multiple databases. For this example to work, your application must be running in a JTA-aware J2EE container.

If you're using some kind of agile programming method, you'll likely run into this kind of scenario. Agile methods suggest that you take simple approaches to a problem, and implement more complex features only when they're needed. Dependency injection makes it much easier to take slightly different versions of application resources and plug them into a given application without major upheaval.

# How do I do that?

In this case, you're going to maintain monetary transaction information in a separate database, rentaBikeAccounts. Whenever users make a reservation, they have to provide a down payment, and you'll transactionally add this amount to the monetaryTransactions table in the new database. Example 7-5 is the script for setting up the new database and table.

**Example 7-5.** rentabike.sql

```
create database rentaBikeAccounts;
use rentabikeAccounts;

create table monetaryTransactions (
    txId int(11) not null auto_increment,
    resId int(11) not null default '0',
    amount double not null default '0',
    `type` varchar(50) not null,
    primary key (txId))
    type=InnoDB;
```

Don't forget that you'll need to set up a user account in MySQL with privileges on the new database:

```
GRANT ALL PRIVILEGES ON rentaBikeAccounts.* TO
'rentaBikeAccounts'@'localhost' WITH GRANT OPTION;
```

We just created a user named rentaBikeAccounts, with complete access to the new database.

Next, Example 7-6 creates a persistent domain class.

**Example 7-6.** MonetaryTransaction.java

```
public class MonetaryTransaction {
    private int txId;
    private int resId;
    private double amount;

    public int getTxId( ) {
        return txId;
    }

    public void setTxId(int txId) {
        this.txId = txId;
    }

    public int getResId( ) {
        return custId;
    }
```

**Example 7-6.** MonetaryTransaction.java (continued)

```java
    public void setResId(int resId) {
        this.resId = resId;
    }

    public double getAmount() {
        return amount;
    }

    public void setAmount(double amount) {
        this.amount = amount;
    }

    public MonetaryTransaction(double amount, int resid) {
        this.resId = resid;
        this.amount = amount;
        this.txId = -1;
    }

    public MonetaryTransaction() {
    this(0.0, 0);
    }
}
```

Map the schema to the class, as in Example 7-7.

**Example 7-7.** MonetaryTransaction.hbm.xml

```xml
<hibernate-mapping>
   <class name="com.springbook.MonetaryTransaction"
      table="monetaryTransactions">
      <id name="txId" column="txid" type="java.lang.Integer"
         unsaved-value="-1">
         <generator class="native"></generator>
      </id>
      <property name="resId" column="resid" type="int"/>
      <property name="amount" column="amount" type="double"/>
   </class>
</hibernate-mapping>
```

To access this new database, you have to configure a second data source and `SessionFactory` in your application configuration. Session factories handle access for to a single database, so you need a new `SessionFactory` for the second one (Example 7-8).

**Example 7-8.** RentABikeApp-Servlet.xml

```xml
<bean id="dataSourceForAccounts"
   class="org.springframework.jdbc.datasource.DriverManagerDataSource">
   <property name="driverClassName">
      <value>com.mysql.jdbc.Driver</value>
   </property>
```

**Example 7-8.** RentABikeApp-Servlet.xml (continued)

```
    <property name="url">
        <value>jdbc:mysql://localhost/justbikes</value>
    </property>
    <property name="username"><value>rentaBikeAccounts</value></property>
</bean>

<bean id="sessionFactoryForAccounts"
    class="org.springframework.orm.hibernate.LocalSessionFactoryBean">
    <property name="dataSource"><ref local="dataSourceForBikes"/></property>
    <property name="mappingResources">
        <list>
            <value>com/springbook/MonetaryTransaction.hbm.xml</value>
        </list>
    </property>
    <property name="hibernateProperties">
        <props>
            <prop key="hibernate.dialect">
                net.sf.hibernate.dialect.MySQLDialect
            </prop>
            <prop key="hibernate.show_sql">false</prop>
        </props>
    </property>
</bean>
```

Unfortunately, you can't use this new SessionFactory directly within the HibRentABike implementation. That's because HibRentABike extends the Spring-provided HibernateDaoSupport class, which uses a single SessionFactory as the backing behind getHibernateTemplate( ). As such, you need a second façade class, this one to model access to this new database through the new SessionFactory (Examples 7-9 and 7-10).

**Example 7-9.** Accounts.java

```
public interface Accounts {
    void addTx(MonetaryTransaction tx);
    MonetaryTransaction getTx(int id);
    List getTxs( );
}
```

**Example 7-10.** RentABikeAccounts.java

```
public class RentABikeAccounts
    extends HibernateDaoSupport
    implements Accounts {

    public void addTx(MonetaryTransaction tx) {
        getHibernateTemplate( ).saveOrUpdate(tx);
    }
```

**Example 7-10.** RentABikeAccounts.java (continued)

```java
    public MonetaryTransaction getTx(int id) {
        return (MonetaryTransaction)getHibernateTemplate( ).
        load(MonetaryTransaction.class, new Integer(id));
    }

    public List getTxs( ) {
        return getHibernateTemplate( ).find("from MonetaryTransaction");
    }
}
```

You need to configure this façade in your application configuration (Example 7-11).

**Example 7-11.** RentABike-servlet.xml

```xml
<bean id="rentaBikeAccountsTarget"
    class="com.springbook.RentABikeAccounts">
    <property name="sessionFactory">
        <ref local="sessionFactoryForAccounts"/>
    </property>
</bean>

<bean id="rentaBikeAccounts"
    class="org.springframework.aop.framework.ProxyFactoryBean">
    <property name="proxyInterfaces">
        <value>com.springbook.Accounts</value>
    </property>
    <property name="interceptorNames">
        <value>transactionInterceptor,rentaBikeAccountsTarget</value>
    </property>
</bean>
```

Finally, use this new functionality within the RentABike façade, which means you'll need to add a setter to RentABike and wire them together in the application context. Example 7-12 shows the additions to HibRentABike.

**Example 7-12.** HibRentABike.java

```java
private Accounts accountsFacade;

public Accounts getAccountsFacade( ) {
    return accountsFacade;
}

public void setAccountsFacade(Accounts accountsFacade) {
    this.accountsFacade = accountsFacade;
}

public void addReservation(Reservation reservation, double amount)
    throws AddReservationException {
```

**Example 7-12.** HibRentABike.java (continued)

```
      try {
        MonetaryTransaction tx = new MonetaryTransaction(amount,
            reservation.getReservationId());
        getHibernateTemplate().saveOrUpdate(reservation);
        accountsFacade.addTx(tx);
      } catch (Exception ex) {
        throw new AddReservationException();
      }
  }
```

Example 7-13 shows the additions to the configuration file.

**Example 7-13.** App-Servlet.xml

```xml
<bean id="rentaBikeTarget" class="com.springbook.HibRentABike">
    <property name="storeName"><value>Bruce's Bikes</value></property>
    <property name="sessionFactory"><ref local="sessionFactory"/></property>
    <property name="accountsFacade">
        <ref local="rentaBikeAccounts"/>
    </property>
</bean>

<bean id="transactionManager"
    class="org.springframework.transaction.jta.JtaTransactionManager">
</bean>

<bean name="transactionInterceptor"
      class="org.springframework.transaction.interceptor.TransactionInterceptor">
    <property name="transactionManager">
        <ref local="transactionManager"/>
    </property>
    <property name="transactionAttributeSource">
      <value>
          com.springbook.RentABike.transferReservation=
              PROPAGATION_REQUIRED,-ReservationTransferException
          com.springbook.RentABike.addReservation=
              PROPAGATION_REQUIRED,-AddReservationException
      </value>
    </property>
</bean>
```

# What just happened?

After adding a second data source, you were able to quickly add XA transactional functionality to the application. Now, whenever the HibRentABike.addReservation() method is called, the application transactionally adds a reservation to the original database and a MonetaryTransaction to the new database. You added a few new classes to the domain model, but mostly this was accomplished through configuration settings. Spring's Hibernate and JTA support handle most of the heavy lifting, and now the application handles multiple physical data stores inside a single distributed transaction.

# Securing Application Servlets

Declarative transactions are the most popular declarative services in Spring, but not the only ones. Spring also allows declarative remoting and declarative security. In this example, you'll use a declarative security service called ACEGI.

## Why do I care?

Since ACEGI is a declarative service, you can use it to secure any method on any bean in the context, without writing extra supportive code. ACEGI also has advanced features that are well beyond most EJB implementations, including the following:

- A robust sign on implementation, based on Yale University's open source Central Authentication Services (CAS)
- An instance based security model
- Pluggable authentication implementations
- HTTP authentication

You can access many of ACEGI's features declaratively. Your POJOs will not be overwhelmed with security code.

## How do I do that?

First, you'll use the servlet-based implementation of ACEGI. This approach uses servlet filters. You'll configure it through a combination of additions to the Spring and `web.xml` configurations. To get going with ACEGI, download the latest version from their web site (*http:// acegisecurity.sourceforge.net/downloads.html*). We used Version 0.6.1. From the `/dist` folder, copy `acegi-security-catalina-server.jar` into the `/server/lib` folder of your Tomcat install. You will also need available to your web application `aopalliance.jar`, `spring.jar`, and `acegi-security-catalina-common.jar`, and `acegi-security.jar`.

Your first implementation will used forms-based authentication to verify users. You have to create a login form that users will be redirected to whenever they attempt to access any of our restricted site pages. This file will be called `acegilogin.jsp`. Its only requirements are that it be a non-restricted page and that it contain a username field and a password field with well-known identifiers. Example 7-14 is acegilogin.jsp.

**Example 7-14.** acegilogin.jsp

```
<%@ taglib prefix='c' uri='http://java.sun.com/jstl/core' %>
<%@ page import="net.sf.acegisecurity.ui.AbstractProcessingFilter,
                 net.sf.acegisecurity.ui.webapp.HttpSessionIntegrationFilter" %>
<%@ page import="net.sf.acegisecurity.AuthenticationException" %>

<h1>Login</h1>
<form action="j_acegi_security_check" method="POST">
Username: <input type="text" name="j_username"><br/>
Password: <input type="password" name="j_password"><br/>
<input type="submit" value="Login">
</form>

<c:choose>
    <c:when test="${not empty param.error}">
        <font color="red">
        Your login attempt was not successful, try again.<BR><BR>
        Reason: <%= ((AuthenticationException) session.getAttribute(
            AbstractProcessingFilter.ACEGI_SECURITY_LAST_EXCEPTION_KEY)).
            getMessage( ) %>
        </font>
    </c:when>
</c:choose>
```

*You must have userid and password fields.*

You should add a special section at the end to display login errors if the user enters invalid credentials. Note that the username field must be called j_username and the password field must be j_password. The ACEGI standard action for the form is j_acegi_security_check, though you could rename it to whatever you like.

Next you have to configure the ACEGI security beans in your Spring configuration (Example 7-15). Although ACEGI provides several ways to authenticate user credentials (via LDAP, a database, external provider, and so on), the easiest way is through a special provider called the InMemoryDaoImpl. This allows you to configure the user credentials in your configuration file.

**Example 7-15.** RentABikeApp-Servlet.xml

```
<bean id="inMemoryDaoImpl"
    class="net.sf.acegisecurity.providers.dao.memory.InMemoryDaoImpl">
        <property name="userMap">
            <value>
            justin=gehtland,ROLE_USER,ROLE_ADMIN
```

**Example 7-15.** RentABikeApp-Servlet.xml (continued)

```
            bruce=tate,ROLE_USER
            </value>
    </property>
</bean>
```

Configure users with username to the left of the equals and a comma-separated list of values to the right. Put the password first. Remaining values are roles for the user. You can choose to use an ACEGI-provided password encoding scheme here that employs MD5 hashing.

To finish the authentication configuration, you have to wrap the InMemoryDaoImpl in a DaoAuthenticationProvider, then feed that provider to a ProviderManager, as in Example 7-16.

**Example 7-16.** RentABikeApp-Servlet.xml

```xml
<bean id="daoAuthenticationProvider"
   class="net.sf.acegisecurity.providers.dao.DaoAuthenticationProvider">
   <property name="authenticationDao">
      <ref local="inMemoryDaoImpl"/>
   </property>
</bean>

<bean id="authenticationManager"
   class="net.sf.acegisecurity.providers.ProviderManager">
   <property name="providers">
      <list>
         <ref local="daoAuthenticationProvider"/>
      </list>
   </property>
</bean>
```

The DaoAuthenticationProvider ACEGI class implements ACEGI's AuthenticationProvider interface. It exposes authentication methods like authenticate and isPasswordCorrect. The ProviderManager simply iterates through a list of AuthenticationProviders to authenticate a given request. In rentaBike, you only have DaoAuthenticationProvider.

Next, you need to tell ACEGI how to determine if a user is authorized to make a specific call (Example 7-17). ACEGI has the notion of DecisionManagers and Voters. Voters are beans that examine credentials and cast votes about access; DecisionManagers collect votes from Voters and determine outcomes. Although you can author your own Voters and DecisionManagers, ACEGI provides a straightforward approach through pre-built classes, the RoleVoter and the AffirmativeBasedDecisionManager.

**Example 7-17.** RentABikeApp-Servlet.xml

```
<bean id="roleVoter" class="net.sf.acegisecurity.vote.RoleVoter"/>

<bean id="httpRequestAccessDecisionManager"
    class="net.sf.acegisecurity.vote.AffirmativeBased">
    <property name="allowIfAllAbstainDecisions"><value>false</value>
    </property>
    <property name="decisionVoters">
        <list>
            <ref local="roleVoter"/>
        </list>
    </property>
</bean>
```

The RoleVoter requires that the roles be configured using some role beginning with ROLE_, like our ROLE_USER role above. The AffirmativeBased DecisionManager asks each configured Voter for its vote, and then permits access if any vote "yes".

Next, you need to configure a FilterSecurityInterceptor that protects access to resources. You configure it to point to your ProviderManager and DecisionManager, then feed it a list of protected resources (Example 7-18).

**Example 7-18.** RentABikeApp-Servlet.xml

```
<bean id="filterInvocationInterceptor"
    class="net.sf.acegisecurity.intercept.web.FilterSecurityInterceptor">
    <property name="authenticationManager">
        <ref local="authenticationManager"/>
    </property>
    <property name="accessDecisionManager">
        <ref local="httpRequestAccessDecisionManager"/>
    </property>
    <property name="objectDefinitionSource">
        <value>
            CONVERT_URL_TO_LOWERCASE_BEFORE_COMPARISON
            \A/.*/*.bikes\Z=ROLE_USER
        </value>
    </property>
</bean>
```

Note the CONVERT_URL_TO_LOWERCASE_BEFORE_COMPARISON directive at the top of our protected resources list. There are other available directives, the most common is PATTERN_TYPE_APACHE_ANT, for Ant-style pattern-matching. The default is regular expression–matching. Your protection list says that any URL anywhere in the application that ends in .bikes (our standard redirect) requires the user to belong to ROLE_USER. You could then add further expressions to the list to require other roles. For example, to lock down a subfolder called admin to users belonging to ROLE_ADMIN, see Example 7-19.

**Example 7-19.** RentABikeApp-Servlet.xml

```
<property name="objectDefinitionSource">
   <value>
      CONVERT_URL_TO_LOWERCASE_BEFORE_COMPARISON
      \A/.*/admin/*.htm\Z=ROLE_ADMIN
      \A/.*/*.bikes\Z=ROLE_USER
   </value>
</property>
```

In the list of protected resources, order is important. ACEGI matches the first role in the list, so if you listed the *admin* folder last, any user of ROLE_USER could access the *admin* folder, which would be *bad*.

Finally, configure the servlet filters themselves (Example 7-20). You will need three: a SecurityEnforcementFilter, an AutoIntegrationFilter, and an AuthenticationProcessingFilter. The enforcement filter uses FilterSecurityInterceptor to determine if access to a resource has been granted, and the AuthenticationProcessingFilter redirects unauthenticated users to the login page. The SecurityEnforcementFilter also needs access to a configured AuthenticationProcessingFilterEntryPoint, which simply stores the URL for the login page and specifies whether it requires HTTPS.

**Example 7-20.** RentABikeApp-Servlet.xml

```
<bean id="securityEnforcementFilter"
   class="net.sf.acegisecurity.intercept.web.SecurityEnforcementFilter">
   <property name="filterSecurityInterceptor">
      <ref local="filterInvocationInterceptor"/>
   </property>
   <property name="authenticationEntryPoint">
      <ref local="authenticationProcessingFilterEntryPoint"/>
   </property>
</bean>

<bean id="authenticationProcessingFilterEntryPoint"
class="net.sf.acegisecurity.ui.webapp.AuthenticationProcessingFilterEntryPoint">
   <property name="loginFormUrl"><value>/acegilogin.jsp</value></property>
   <property name="forceHttps"><value>false</value></property>
</bean>

<bean id="authenticationProcessingFilter"
   class="net.sf.acegisecurity.ui.webapp.AuthenticationProcessingFilter">
   <property name="authenticationManager">
      <ref local="authenticationManager"/>
   </property>
```

Example 7-20. RentABikeApp-Servlet.xml (continued)

```
    <property name="authenticationFailureUrl">
        <value>/acegilogin.jsp?login_error=1</value>
    </property>
    <property name="defaultTargetUrl"><value>/</value></property>
    <property name="filterProcessesUrl">
        <value>/j_acegi_security_check</value>
    </property>
</bean>
<bean id="autoIntegrationFilter"
    class="net.sf.acegisecurity.ui.AutoIntegrationFilter"></bean>
```

The AuthenticationProcessingFilter requires four properties:

*authenticationManager*

Provides the AuthenticationProvider that will authenticate the user.

*authenticationFailureUrl*

Redirects when the user enters invalid credentials.

*defaultTargetUrl*

Redirects if a user accesses the login page directly instead of being redirected from a protected URL.

*filterProcessingUrl*

Specifies the target of the login page's form.

Last but not least, you have to modify the web.xml file to enable the required filters (Example 7-21).

Example 7-21. web.xml

```
<filter>
    <filter-name>Acegi Authentication Processing Filter</filter-name>
    <filter-class>net.sf.acegisecurity.util.FilterToBeanProxy</filter-class>
    <init-param>
        <param-name>targetClass</param-name>
        <param-value>
            net.sf.acegisecurity.ui.webapp.AuthenticationProcessingFilter
        </param-value>
    </init-param>
</filter>

<filter>
    <filter-name>
        Acegi Security System for Spring Auto Integration Filter
    </filter-name>
    <filter-class>net.sf.acegisecurity.util.FilterToBeanProxy</filter-class>
    <init-param>
        <param-name>targetClass</param-name>
        <param-value>
            net.sf.acegisecurity.ui.AutoIntegrationFilter
        </param-value>
```

**Example 7-21.** web.xml (continued)

```
      </init-param>
   </filter>

   <filter>
      <filter-name>Acegi HTTP Request Security Filter</filter-name>
      <filter-class>net.sf.acegisecurity.util.FilterToBeanProxy</filter-class>
      <init-param>
         <param-name>targetClass</param-name>
         <param-value>
            net.sf.acegisecurity.intercept.web.SecurityEnforcementFilter
         </param-value>
      </init-param>
   </filter>

   <filter-mapping>
      <filter-name>Acegi Authentication Processing Filter</filter-name>
      <url-pattern>/*</url-pattern>
   </filter-mapping>

   <filter-mapping>
      <filter-name>
         Acegi Security System for Spring Auto Integration Filter
      </filter-name>
      <url-pattern>/*</url-pattern>
   </filter-mapping>

   <filter-mapping>
      <filter-name>Acegi HTTP Request Security Filter</filter-name>
      <url-pattern>/*</url-pattern>
   </filter-mapping>
```

Now, when you run it, ACEGI will force you to authenticate. Example 7-22 is the log output from attempting to access the root of the site, */bikes.htm*.

**Example 7-22.** rentabike.log

```
2004-11-28 14:05:13,532 DEBUG [net.sf.acegisecurity.ui.AbstractIntegrationFilter]
- Authentication not added to ContextHolder (could not extract an authentication
object from the container which is an instance of Authentication)
2004-11-28 14:05:13,532 DEBUG [net.sf.acegisecurity.intercept.web.
RegExpBasedFilterInvocationDefinitionMap] - Converted URL to lowercase, from:
'org.apache.coyote.tomcat5.CoyoteRequestFacade@3290aa'; to: '/bikes.htm'
2004-11-28 14:05:13,532 DEBUG [net.sf.acegisecurity.intercept.web.
RegExpBasedFilterInvocationDefinitionMap] - Candidate is: '/bikes.htm'; pattern
is \A/.*/*.htm\Z; matched=true
2004-11-28 14:05:13,532 DEBUG [net.sf.acegisecurity.intercept.
AbstractSecurityInterceptor] - Secure object: FilterInvocation: URL: /bikes.htm;
ConfigAttributes: [ROLE_USER]
```

**Example 7-22.** rentabike.log (continued)

```
2004-11-28 14:05:13,533 DEBUG [net.sf.acegisecurity.intercept.web.
SecurityEnforcementFilter] - Authentication failed - adding target URL to
Session: http://localhost:8080/rentabike/bikes.htm
net.sf.acegisecurity.AuthenticationCredentialsNotFoundException: A valid
SecureContext was not provided in the RequestContext
    at net.sf.acegisecurity.intercept.AbstractSecurityInterceptor.
interceptor(AbstractSecurityInterceptor.java:280)
    ...etc.
```

```
2004-11-28 14:05:13,534 DEBUG [net.sf.acegisecurity.ui.webapp.
AuthenticationProcessingFilterEntryPoint] - Redirecting to: http://localhost:
8080/rentabike/acegilogin.jsp
2004-11-28 14:05:13,534 DEBUG [net.sf.acegisecurity.ui.AbstractIntegrationFilter]
- ContextHolder does not contain any authentication information
...[other log entries]   net.sf.acegisecurity.providers.dao.event.
AuthenticationSuccessEvent[source=net.sf.acegisecurity.providers.
UsernamePasswordAuthenticationToken@514faa: Username: bruce; Password:
[PROTECTED]; Authenticated: false; Details: 127.0.0.1; Not granted any
authorities]
```

```
2004-11-28 14:05:18,495 INFO [net.sf.acegisecurity.providers.dao.event.
LoggerListener] - Authentication success for user: bruce; details: 127.0.0.1
2004-11-28 14:05:18,495 DEBUG [net.sf.acegisecurity.ui.AbstractProcessingFilter]
- Authentication success: net.sf.acegisecurity.providers.
UsernamePasswordAuthenticationToken@453924: Username: bruce; Password:
[PROTECTED]; Authenticated: false; Details: 127.0.0.1; Granted Authorities: ROLE_
USER
```

```
2004-11-28 14:05:18,495 DEBUG [net.sf.acegisecurity.ui.AbstractProcessingFilter]
- Redirecting to target URL from HTTP Session (or default): http://localhost:
8080/rentabike/bikes.htm
```

As you can see from the log, the request for */bikes.htm* is matched against our rule and ACEGI knows that only users belonging to ROLE_USER can access it. ACEGI checks the Context for an Authentication object, finds none, so redirects the user to */acegilogin.jsp*, but first captures the original target URL in the HttpSession. After the user authenticates successfully, ACEGI automatically redirects the user to the original target. This time, when ACEGI attempts to verify the user, the Authentication object is already in the session, permission is granted, and normal Spring dispatching takes over.

## What just happened?

You just saw one of three ways that ACEGI can secure an application. This is the most straightforward method, with the least amount of control. The servlet filters–based approach uses J2EE servlet filters to intercept control before the initial Spring dispatcher is called. Then, ACEGI allows access if the user has appropriate credentials.

# Securing Application Methods

In this lab, you'll learn to use a different kind of security. You'll secure a method on a bean instead of a servlet. This type of security is still declarative, but it's a little more involved.

EJB security works by assigning users roles, giving permissions to those roles, and then assigning permissions to individual methods. In Spring, to use that model, you'll want to secure a method on a bean in the context, instead. In most cases, you'll want to secure the methods on your façade layer—in your case, the rentaBike bean.

## How do I do that?

Method-based security relies on user roles, just like servlet-based security does (Example 7-23). You have already established two users with different roles in the previous lab.

**Example 7-23.** RentABikeApp-Servlet.xml

```
<bean id="inMemoryDaoImpl"
    class="net.sf.acegisecurity.providers.dao.memory.InMemoryDaoImpl">
    <property name="userMap">
        <value>
            justin=gehtland,ROLE_USER,ROLE_ADMIN
            bruce=tate,ROLE_USER
        </value>
    </property>
</bean>
```

To establish access rules for methods on a bean, you have to create an instance of ACEGI's MethodSecurityInterceptor (Example 7-24). For this application, you will want to secure methods on the façade layer that controls your data model. The interceptor needs references to a ProviderManager and a DecisionManager, just like the FilterSecurityInterceptor in the previous lab did. Similarly, it will have a property called objectDefinitionSource that lists the methods on the beans that need to be secured, and what roles have access to them. For example, all members of ROLE_USER should be able to read data from the database, but only members of ROLE_ADMIN should be able to save, update, or delete.

**Example 7-24.** RentABikeApp-Servlet.xml

```
<bean id="bikeRentalSecurity"
    class="net.sf.acegisecurity.intercept.method.MethodSecurityInterceptor">
```

**Example 7-24.** RentABikeApp-Servlet.xml (continued)

```
<property name="authenticationManager">
    <ref local="authenticationManager"/>
</property>
<property name="accessDecisionManager">
    <ref local="httpRequestAccessDecisionManager"/>
</property>
<property name="objectDefinitionSource">
    <value>
        com.springbook.RentABike.saveBike=ROLE_ADMIN
        com.springbook.RentABike.deleteBike=ROLE_ADMIN
        com.springbook.RentABike.saveCustomer=ROLE_ADMIN
        com.springbook.RentABike.deleteCustomer=ROLE_ADMIN
    </value>
</property>
</bean>
```

*ACEGI will secure these methods.*

To wire up the interceptor, you have to create a proxy around the rentaBike controller, just like we did in Chapter 6. First, make sure that your actual BikeStore is configured properly (Example 7-25).

**Example 7-25.** RentABikeApp-Servlet.xml

```
<bean id="rentaBikeTarget" class="com.springbook.HibRentABike">
    <property name="storeName"><value>Bruce's Bikes</value></property>
    <property name="sessionFactory"><ref local="sessionFactory"/></property>
    <property name="transactionManager">
        <ref local="transactionManager"/>
    </property>
</bean>
```

Then, wrap it in a Spring interceptor, using the MethodSecurity-Interceptor as the filter (Example 7-26).

**Example 7-26.** RentABikeApp-Servlet.xml

```
<bean id="rentaBike"
    class="org.springframework.aop.framework.ProxyFactoryBean">
    <property name="proxyInterfaces">
        <value>com.springbook.RentABike</value>
    </property>
    <property name="interceptorNames">
        <list>
            <idref local="bikeRentalSecurity"/>
            <idref local="rentaBikeTarget"/>
        </list>
    </property>
</bean>
```

Now, try to sign on as a user belonging to ROLE_ADMIN. Example 7-27 is the log output when you attempt to issue a saveBike command.

**Example 7-27.** rentabike.log

```
2004-11-29 10:41:39,906 DEBUG [net.sf.acegisecurity.intercept.
AbstractSecurityInterceptor] - Secure object: Invocation: method=[public abstract
void com.springbook.RentABike.saveBike(com.springbook.Bike)] args=[Ljava.lang.
Object;@68b9f] target is of class [com.springbook.HibRentABike];
ConfigAttributes: [ROLE_ADMIN]
2004-11-29 10:41:39,906 DEBUG [net.sf.acegisecurity.providers.ProviderManager] -
Authentication attempt using net.sf.acegisecurity.providers.dao.
DaoAuthenticationProvider
2004-11-29 10:41:39,906 DEBUG [org.springframework.web.context.support.
XmlWebApplicationContext] - Publishing event in context [XmlWebApplicationContext
for namespace 'rentaBikeApp-servlet']:
```
**net.sf.acegisecurity.providers.dao.event.AuthenticationSuccessEvent[source=net.
sf.acegisecurity.providers.UsernamePasswordAuthenticationToken@d92c96: Username:
justin; Password: [PROTECTED]; Authenticated: false; Details: 127.0.0.1; Granted
Authorities: ROLE_USER, ROLE_ADMIN]**
```
2004-11-29 10:41:39,906 INFO [net.sf.acegisecurity.providers.dao.event.
LoggerListener] - Authentication success for user: justin; details: 127.0.0.1
...[call then proceeds as normal]
```

*This one passed the authentication test.*

If you log out and log back in as a user NOT in the ROLE_ADMIN role,
Example 7-28 is the log output.

**Example 7-28.** rentabike.log

```
2004-11-29 11:04:59,240 DEBUG [net.sf.acegisecurity.intercept.
AbstractSecurityInterceptor] - Secure object: Invocation: method=[public abstract
void com.springbook.RentABike.saveBike(com.springbook.Bike)] args=[Ljava.lang.
Object;@26bd42] target is of class [com.springbook.HibRentABike];
ConfigAttributes: [ROLE_ADMIN]
2004-11-29 11:04:59,240 DEBUG [net.sf.acegisecurity.providers.ProviderManager] -
Authentication attempt using net.sf.acegisecurity.providers.dao.
DaoAuthenticationProvider
2004-11-29 11:04:59,240 DEBUG [org.springframework.web.context.support.
XmlWebApplicationContext] - Publishing event in context [XmlWebApplicationContext
for namespace 'rentaBikeApp-servlet']: net.sf.acegisecurity.providers.dao.event.
AuthenticationSuccessEvent[source=net.sf.acegisecurity.providers.
UsernamePasswordAuthenticationToken@c91c22: Username: bruce; Password:
[PROTECTED]; Authenticated: false; Details: 127.0.0.1; Granted Authorities: ROLE_
USER]
2004-11-29 11:04:59,241 INFO [net.sf.acegisecurity.providers.dao.event.
LoggerListener] - Authentication success for user: bruce; details: 127.0.0.1
2004-11-29 11:04:59,241 DEBUG [org.springframework.web.context.support.
XmlWebApplicationContext] - Publishing event in context [Root
XmlWebApplicationContext]:
```
**net.sf.acegisecurity.providers.dao.event.AuthenticationSuccessEvent[source=net.
sf.acegisecurity.providers.UsernamePasswordAuthenticationToken@c91c22: Username:
bruce; Password: [PROTECTED]; Authenticated: false; Details: 127.0.0.1; Granted
Authorities: ROLE_USER]**
```

2004-11-29 11:04:59,241 INFO [net.sf.acegisecurity.providers.dao.event.
LoggerListener] - Authentication success for user: bruce; details: 127.0.0.1
```

*In this case, authentication fails.*

**Example 7-28.** rentabike.log (continued)

```
2004-11-29 11:04:59,241 DEBUG [net.sf.acegisecurity.intercept.
AbstractSecurityInterceptor] - Authenticated: net.sf.acegisecurity.providers.
UsernamePasswordAuthenticationToken@537945: Username: bruce; Password:
[PROTECTED]; Authenticated: true; Details: 127.0.0.1; Granted Authorities: ROLE_
USER
2004-11-29 11:04:59,241 ERROR [org.springframework.web.servlet.DispatcherServlet]
- Could not complete request
net.sf.acegisecurity.AccessDeniedException: Access is denied.
    at net.sf.acegisecurity.vote.AffirmativeBased.decide(AffirmativeBased.java:
86)
ETC.
2004-11-29 11:04:59,243 DEBUG [org.springframework.web.context.support.
XmlWebApplicationContext] - Publishing event in context [XmlWebApplicationContext
for namespace 'rentaBikeApp-servlet']: RequestHandledEvent: url=[/rentabike/
editBike.htm]; time=[5ms]; client=[127.0.0.1]; method=[POST];
servlet=[rentaBikeApp]; session=[029AB8AD12ED146A4356817166C38083]; user=[null];
status=[failed: net.sf.acegisecurity.AccessDeniedException: Access is denied.]
2004-11-29 11:04:59,243 DEBUG [org.springframework.web.context.support.
XmlWebApplicationContext] - Publishing event in context [Root
XmlWebApplicationContext]: RequestHandledEvent: url=[/rentabike/editBike.htm];
time=[5ms]; client=[127.0.0.1]; method=[POST]; servlet=[rentaBikeApp];
session=[029AB8AD12ED146A4356817166C38083]; user=[null]; status=[failed: net.sf.
acegisecurity.AccessDeniedException: Access is denied.]
2004-11-29 11:04:59,243 DEBUG [net.sf.acegisecurity.intercept.web.
SecurityEnforcementFilter] - Access is denied - sending back forbidden response
2004-11-29 11:04:59,243 DEBUG [net.sf.acegisecurity.ui.AbstractIntegrationFilter]
- Updating container with new Authentication object, and then removing
Authentication from ContextHolder
```

## What just happened?

The ACEGI model uses interceptors. These interceptors map credentials (or roles) onto an individual user when the user authenticates. ACEGI stores this information in its authentication engine, and lets you, or an interceptor, query this information.

Next, ACEGI stores a map of permissions on each role. Then, when you proxy an interface, you specify what credentials are required to do a particular thing, like fire a method. Like the other services in this chapter, these work declaratively.

## What about...

...instance-based security? EJB security often breaks down because guarding an individual method is not enough. You don't care whether a manager wants to retrieve invoices. You care which invoices the manager wants to retrieve. He should only have access to the invoices for employees in his department.

ACEGI provides instance-based security. You can attach ACLs (access control lists) to individual instances, just as you attached permissions to roles. ACEGI provides a mapping mechanism to do this. You can assign AclEntries to domain instances, then use an AclManager to look up AclEntries from a given domain instance. AccessDecisionManagers then decide if the current user has appropriate permissions based on the AclEntries.

# Building a Test-Friendly Interceptor

In this example, you'll learn how to build interceptors that do nothing but improve your ability to test code. Usually, a transaction interceptor does three things:

1. Begins a transaction when a method starts.
2. Rolls back a transaction when an exception is thrown.
3. Commits the transaction when a method completes.

Of course, that's what you usually want to happen. Test cases are different animals, though. They're responsible for putting conditions back to the state where they were before a test case was fired, and they need to execute quickly.

For a test case, often it makes sense to replace the third step. You may instead want the transaction to roll back after the method completes. That way, you remove one of the most expensive database steps (the commit), and you also restore the database state to what it was before you executed the transaction.

## How do I do that?

In Spring, it's easy to build this type of behavior into an interceptor, because you can build a custom interceptor. Example 7-29 shows the code for a transaction interceptor that rolls back.

**Example 7-29.** TestTxInterceptor.java

```
public class TestTxInterceptor implements MethodInterceptor {
    private PlatformTransactionManager platformTransactionManager;

    public PlatformTransactionManager getPlatformTransactionManager() {
        return platformTransactionManager;
    }
```

**Example 7-29.** TestTxInterceptor.java (continued)

```java
  public void setPlatformTransactionManager(PlatformTransactionManager
    platformTransactionManager) {
      this.platformTransactionManager = platformTransactionManager;
  }

  public Object invoke(MethodInvocation methodInvocation)
    throws Throwable {
    DefaultTransactionDefinition def =
      new DefaultTransactionDefinition( );
    def.setPropagationBehavior(TransactionDefinition.
      PROPAGATION_REQUIRED);
    TransactionStatus status =
      platformTransactionManager.getTransaction(def);

    Object results = null;
    try {
        results = methodInvocation.proceed( );
    } finally {
        platformTransactionManager.rollback(status);
    }
    return results;
  }
}
```

Next, Example 7-30 shows the configuration of the context.

**Example 7-30.** RentABikeApp-Servlet.xml

```xml
<bean id="transactionManager"
   class="org.springframework.orm.hibernate.HibernateTransactionManager">
   <property name="sessionFactory"><ref local="sessionFactory"/></property>
</bean>

<bean id="testTxInterceptor"
   class="com.springbook.interceptors.TestTxInterceptor">
   <property name="platformTransactionManager">
     <ref local="transactionManager"/>
   </property>
</bean>

<bean id="rentaBike"
   class="org.springframework.aop.framework.ProxyFactoryBean">
   <property name="proxyInterfaces">
     <value>com.springbook.RentABike</value>
   </property>
   <property name="interceptorNames">
       <list>
          <idref local="bikeRentalSecurity"/>
          <idref local="testTxInterceptor"/>
          <idref local="rentaBikeTarget"/>
       </list>
```

**Chapter 7: Transactions and Security**

**Example 7-30.** RentABikeApp-Servlet.xml (continued)

```
    </property>
</bean>
```

Now, you can write any JUnit tests you want against the façade layer, testing reads and writes, testing for appropriate security filtering, and so on, without worrying about changing the database. When running the unit tests, use a version of the configuration file that assigns the interceptor, and leave out the interceptor in a deployment scenario.

# What just happened?

The typical JUnit flow works like this:

- `setUp` prepares the system for a test case. In our `setUp` method, we do all of the work that's common across the databases.
- A series of individual tests then follow. In our case, we slightly change the flow, in order to call all of the methods within a method that uses the Spring context.

`tearDown` then does all cleanup. For database tests, the `tearDown` can be particularly expensive, because it's got to restore the test data to a usable state for other test cases. (An alternative approach is the reset the database to a known good state in every `setUp` method. If the set of test data is small enough, this is a safer approach. The larger the set of test data, the more likely it is that you will want to use `tearDown` to undo test changes instead of `setUp` to recreate the full database.) A test changes something in the database, verifies the results, and then repeats. Notice also that all of the database access is in a central method. That makes it easy to bracket the method with declarative transactions.

Now look at the context. This is a case where you're actually proxying the test code to add some behavior that makes testing easier. That's using the power of Spring to build a much better test. In the next chapter, you'll look into a few more services, like remoting and messaging.

# Messaging and Remoting

In early 2001, the sun was shining, but I got a call from another kayaker named Steve Daniel saying that North Grape Creek was runnable, but below flood stage. It had never been run before. It required access through private property, and had to be at a perfect level: high enough to run, and low enough to navigate the many low-water crossings that dot the Texas country side. I wondered how Steve timed it perfectly.

If you've followed my books and other articles, you may be intrigued that a whitewater kayaker can find enough runnable water in a dry state like Texas. In truth, there's nowhere near enough water near Austin to support my habit. I've got to chase the storms, and rely on the Internet. I can use the United States Geological Service (USGS) to track stream and river flows across the United States. I can tell when an obscure stream like North Grape is in flood, or just below flood stage. Since I can make such requests with a browser, I don't need to inundate people like dam operators with requests, and they don't have to respond. As a result, USGS has a group of unlikely satisfied customers, and we have an unexpected source of data from the United States government. After Steve charmed the local land owners, he found North Grape by watching the right pages on the Internet. Over the years, I've gotten many calls for similar trips, and Steve has written a book on Texas whitewater. Building remote access into existing applications is the subject of this chapter.

## Sending Email Messages

In Chapter 6, you learned how to attach behaviors to a bean. You built an example to write a message to a database whenever an exception was thrown. An email message would be more useful. Let's use Spring's email abstraction to send an email message to a user when something breaks.

# How do I do that?

Spring provides a set of services to help you quickly send email messages. You'll need to use three classes to get the support:

- The `SimpleMailMessage` class is a value object that has the mail properties that you'll need, such as subject, body, to, from, and cc properties.
- The `MailException` is thrown when something breaks.
- The `MailSender` interface and `JavaMailSender` provide Spring's implementation to send messages. You will, of course, need to configure a mail client.

First, you'll need to configure a simple message. Do that in the context, like in Example 8-1.

**Example 8-1.** RentABikeApp-servlet.xml

```
<bean id="mailMessage" class="org.springframework.mail.SimpleMailMessage">
    <property name="to"><value>itsupport@rentabike.com</value></property>
    <property name="from">
        <value>problems@rentabike.com</value>
    </property>
    <property name="subject"><value>An error occurred</value></property>
    <property name="text">
        <value>There was a problem in the application.</value>
    </property>
</bean>
```

*When you run this example, you'll want to fill in valid to and from email messages.*

Next, you'll want to configure a sender. You'll use the sender that's packaged with the Spring framework. All you need to do is configure it in the context (Example 8-2).

**Example 8-2.** RentABikeApp-servlet.xml

```
<bean id="mailSender"
    class="org.springframework.mail.javamail.JavaMailSenderImpl">
    <property name="host"><value>mail.rentabike.com</value></property>
</bean>
```

Finally, you'll need to write a business method. Change the advisor that you made in Chapter 6 (in the "Advising Exceptions" example) to use the new mail client, as in Example 8-3.

**Example 8-3.** ExceptionInterceptor.java

```
private MailSender mailSender;
private SimpleMailMessage mailMessage;
```

*These set set with dependency injection.*

**Example 8-3.** ExceptionInterceptor.java (continued)

```java
public class ExceptionInterceptor implements ThrowsAdvice {
    private MailSender mailSender;
    private SimpleMailMessage mailMessage;

    public SimpleMailMessage getMailMessage() {
        return mailMessage;
    }

    public void setMailMessage(SimpleMailMessage mailMessage) {
        this.mailMessage = mailMessage;
    }

    public MailSender getMailSender() {
        return mailSender;
    }

    public void setMailSender(MailSender mailSender) {
        this.mailSender = mailSender;
    }

            try {
                    mailMessage.setText(ex.getMessage());
                    mailSender.send(mailMessage);
            } catch (Exception mex) {
                    // handle mail error
            }
    }
}
```

Next, you'll have to configure the advisor, as in Example 8-4.

**Example 8-4.** RentABikeApp-servlet.xml

```xml
<bean id="exceptionInterceptor"
   class="com.springbook.interceptors.ExceptionInterceptor">
    <property name="mailSender"><ref local="mailSender"/></property>
    <property name="mailMessage"><ref local="mailMessage"/></property>
</bean>

<bean id="rentaBike"
   class="org.springframework.aop.framework.ProxyFactoryBean">

    <property name="proxyInterfaces">
      <value>com.springbook.RentABike</value>
    </property>
    <property name="interceptorNames">
      <list>
        <value>exceptionInterceptor</value>
        <value>transactionInterceptor</value>
        <value>rentaBikeTarget</value>
      </list>
```

**Example 8-4.** RentABikeApp-servlet.xml (continued)

```
   </property>
</bean>
```

Now, do something that will cause an exception. For example, shut down the database while the application is running. The JDBC layer should fire an exception next time you try to access the database, which in turn should fire an email message.

## What just happened?

If you'll recall, in Chapter 6 you created an interceptor to log a message. You're using the same advisor. Here's what your code did:

- You changed your advisor to use the Spring email client. You injected the value of the email server and set up a simple message in the context.

- You configured a proxy to intercept calls to the rentABike target. You specified three interceptors, one of which is the new exception handler.

- The proxy calls the interceptor chain whenever a specified method throws any exception. You then configured the interceptor to point to all methods on the rentABike target, and added it to the context.

When you ran the code and coerced an exception, the proxy intercepted the exception, and then notified all of the interceptors in the chain for that method. Your interceptor got fired, and sent the email message.

# Remoting

Remoting is one of the core features of EJB session beans. As a result, with declarative transactions, it's often used to justify the use of EJB, where it may not otherwise apply. In this lab, you'll learn how to do remoting declaratively—by writing configuration instead of any additional code—without EJB. In this example, you'll be able to use Spring's remoting service to access the business logic directly to get all of the bikes in the database over the internet.

Spring supports three kinds of HTTP services: Hessian, Burlap, and HTTP invokers. RMI is a favorite Java remoting technology, but you've got to open an additional port on your firewall, unless you're tunneling. The nice thing about HTTP protocols is that you are using the web's standard communication protocol, so you need not open up your system to do anything beyond what you've to do anyway to support the internet. For starters, you will provide remote support to the façade through HTTP invokers.

## How do I do that?

Most declarative remoting services work by using proxies. For this application, you'll configure remoting so that other applications can access our façade. You're going to need to prepare a client and a server. To prepare the server, you need to set up a second servlet for the remoting services. In the web.xml file, add the servlet definition from Example 8-5.

**Example 8-5.** web.xml

```
<servlet>
   <servlet-name>remoting</servlet-name>
   <servlet-class>
      org.springframework.web.servlet.DispatcherServlet
   </servlet-class>
   <load-on-startup>2</load-on-startup>
</servlet>

<servlet-mapping>
    <servlet-name>remoting</servlet-name>
    <url-pattern>/remoting/*</url-pattern>
</servlet-mapping>
```

Then, create a new servlet configuration file for the new servlet called *remoting-servlet.xml*, as in Example 8-6.

**Example 8-6.** remoting-servlet.xml

```
<?xml version="1.0" encoding="UTF-8"?>
<!DOCTYPE beans PUBLIC "-//SPRING//DTD BEAN//EN" "http://www.springframework.org/
dtd/spring-beans.dtd">
<beans>
    <bean name="/RentABike"
       class="org.springframework.httpinvoker.HttpInvokerExporter">
       <property name="service"><ref bean="rentaBike"/></property>
       <property name="serviceInterface">
           <value>com.springbook.RentABike</value>
       </property>
    </bean>
</beans>
```

On the client side, you'll proxy the façade. Example 8-7 shows the code to configure the client.

**Example 8-7.** RentABikeApp-servlet.xml

```xml
<bean id="rentabikeHttpProxy"
class="org.springframework.remoting.httpinvoker.HttpInvokerProxyFactoryBean">
    <property name="serviceUrl">
        <value>http://YOUR_HOST:8080/RentABike/remoting/RentABike</value>
    </property>
    <property name="serviceInterface">
        <value>com.springbook.RentABike</value>
    </property>
</bean>
```

Now, create a test case like Example 8-8. It should simply get the bikes in the store.

**Example 8-8.** RemotingTest.java

```java
public class RemotingTest extends TestCase {
    private ApplicationContext ctx;
    private RentABike rental = null;

    public void setUp() throws Exception {
        ctx = new FileSystemXmlApplicationContext(
                "/war/WEB-INF/bikeRentalApp-servlet.xml");
        rental = (RentABike)ctx.getBean("rentabikeHttpProxy");
    }

    public void testRemoting() throws Exception {
        Bike b = rental.getBike(1);
        assertNotNull(b);
        //etc.
    }
}
```

Run the test on the client to make sure things are working. You should be able to load and test the properties of any object available from the façade.

# What just happened?

Let's start the flow at the test case. The test case loads the rentabikeHttpProxy bean from the context. As you know by now, the bike store isn't the true implementation. It's just a proxy. When the test case invokes the getBikes method on the rentabikeHttpProxy, the proxy fires an interceptor, which serializes the parameters and sends the request to the server over HTTP.

On the server side, you've exported the service. The servlet engine forwards the request to Spring, which invokes the object under test. The server code returns a list of bikes. Spring's remoting service serializes that list and sends them to the client proxy, which then returns them to the test case.

## What about...

...other remoting services, like Hessian, Burlap, and RMI? Of course, one of the core problems with EJB remoting was that you could not decouple the remoting service from the container. For better or worse, you were stuck with RMI. That's fine, unless you want to remote to clients written in another language, or run over a firewall without opening another port or tunneling.

Spring's HTTP invokers are a good choice for Java over HTTP, but keep in mind that they rely on Java serialization, so they are not necessarily a good choice for cross-language remoting. Hessian and Burlap are remoting services that use a language-neutral representation of the objects. Although the non-Java support is limited in some ways (like for working with proxied objects), you generally do not need sophisticated support when you're remoting across languages.

# Working with JMS

In this example, you'll learn how to communicate asynchronously with JMS. You'll send a new reservation to the billing system, so that the system can bill the customer. We'll focus on billing (the producer side of the equation), but Spring 1.2 intends to support a robust, pooled, and transactional message consumer architecture as well.

Many architects have hailed JMS as one of the best J2EE specifications. It provides a clean separation between the specification interface and pluggable implementations. It provides for a variety of payload structures, and distinct messaging models for peer-to-peer communication and publish-subscribe style communication. In this section, you're going to integrate JMS with Spring.

## How do I do that?

The first job is to configure JMS. To do so, you'll need a JMS provider. We chose ActiveMQ (*http://activemq.codehaus.org*) because it is open source and its authors have provided excellent Spring support, but other implementations should work as well. Download the application, and then launch the JMS provider by navigating to the */bin* folder and issuing the `activemq` command.

In the context, you'll need to configure a connection factory to manage the JMS connection, as in Example 8-9. Point the `brokerURL` to the MQ machine and port.

**Example 8-9.** RentABikeApp-servlet.xml

```xml
<bean id="jmsConnFactory" class="org.codehaus.activemq.
ActiveMQConnectionFactory">
    <property name="brokerURL">
        <value>tcp://yourMqHost:yourMqPort</value>
    </property>
</bean>
```

Next, you'll need a JMS transaction manager, which plugs into the Spring transaction architecture (Example 8-10).

**Example 8-10.** RentABikeApp-servlet.xml

```xml
<bean id="jmsTxManager" class="org.springframework.jms.connection.
JmsTransactionManager">
    <property name="connectionFactory">
        <ref local="jmsConnFactory"/>
    </property>
</bean>
```

You'll also need to create your consumer method. It's going to use a JMS template. Call it `BillingManager`, and then front it with a façade. This class will use a JMS template (Example 8-11).

**Example 8-11.** RentABikeApp-servlet.xml

```xml
<bean id="billingJmsTemplate" class="org.springframework.jms.core.JmsTemplate">
    <property name="connectionFactory">
        <ref local="jmsConnFactory"/>
    </property>
</bean>
```

You'll need to change the façade to notify the queue manager whenever you create a new reservation (Example 8-12).

**Example 8-12.** HibRentABike.java

```java
public void addReservation(Reservation reservation, double amount)
    throws AddReservationException {
    try {
        MonetaryTransaction tx = new MonetaryTransaction(amount,
            reservation.getReservationId());
        getHibernateTemplate().saveOrUpdate(reservation);
        accountsFacade.addTx(tx);
        jmsTemplate.send("billingQueue", new MessageCreator() {
            public Message createMessage(javax.jms.Session session)
```

**Example 8-12.** HibRentABike.java (continued)

```
            throws JMSException {
            return session.createTextMessage("New Reservation: " +
                reservation.toString( ));
        }
      });
  } catch (Exception ex) {
     throw new AddReservationException( );
  }
}
```

Finally, wire it into your façade with a new method and dependency injection. Example 8-13 shows the new property on the façade.

**Example 8-13.** HibRentABike.java

```java
private JmsTemplate jmsTemplate;

public JmsTemplate getJmsTemplate( ) {
   return jmsTemplate;
}

public void setJmsTemplate(JmsTemplate jmsTemplate) {
   this.jmsTemplate = jmsTemplate;
}
```

And Example 8-14 gives the modification to the façade's configuration.

**Example 8-14.** RentABikeApp-servlet.xml

```xml
<bean id="rentaBikeTarget" class="com.springbook.HibRentABike">
   <property name="storeName"><value>Bruce's Bikes</value></property>
   <property name="sessionFactory"><ref local="sessionFactory"/></property>
   <property name="transactionManager">
      <ref local="transactionManager"/>
   </property>
   <property name="jmsTemplate">
      <ref local="billingJmsTemplate"/>
   </property>
</bean>
```

Example 8-15 is a standalone consumer that requires a JNDI-aware container to find and observe the queue. Alternatively, you could use the ConsumerTool in ActiveMQ's */example* folder to watch the messages as they are created.

**Example 8-15.** StandaloneListener.java

```java
import javax.jms.JMSException;
import javax.jms.Message;
import javax.jms.Queue;
```

**Example 8-15.** StandaloneListener.java (continued)

```java
import javax.jms.QueueConnection;
import javax.jms.QueueConnectionFactory;
import javax.jms.QueueReceiver;
import javax.jms.QueueSession;
import javax.jms.Session;
import javax.jms.TextMessage;
import javax.naming.Context;
import javax.naming.InitialContext;
import javax.naming.NamingException;

public class StandaloneListener {

    public static void main(String[] args) {
        String queueName = "billingQueue";
        Context jndiContext = null;
        QueueConnectionFactory queueConnectionFactory = null;
        QueueConnection queueConnection = null;
        QueueSession queueSession = null;
        Queue queue = null;
        QueueReceiver queueReceiver = null;
        TextMessage message = null;

        try {
            jndiContext = new InitialContext();
        }
        catch (NamingException e) {
            System.out.println("Could not create JNDI API " +
                    "context: " + e.toString());
            System.exit(1);
        }

        try {
            queueConnectionFactory = (QueueConnectionFactory)
                    jndiContext.lookup("QueueConnectionFactory");
            queue = (Queue) jndiContext.lookup(queueName);
        }
        catch (NamingException e) {
            System.out.println("JNDI API lookup failed: " +
                    e.toString());
            System.exit(1);
        }

        try {
            queueConnection =
                    queueConnectionFactory.createQueueConnection();
            queueSession =
                    queueConnection.createQueueSession(false,
                            Session.AUTO_ACKNOWLEDGE);
            queueReceiver = queueSession.createReceiver(queue);
            queueConnection.start();
            while (true) {
                Message m = queueReceiver.receive(1);
```

**Example 8-15.** StandaloneListener.java (continued)

```
                if (m != null) {
                    if (m instanceof TextMessage) {
                        message = (TextMessage) m;
                        System.out.println("Reading message: " +
                                message.getText());
                    }
                    else {
                        break;
                    }
                }
            }
        }
        catch (JMSException e) {
            System.out.println("Exception occurred: " +
                    e.toString());
        }
        finally {
            if (queueConnection != null) {
                try {
                    queueConnection.close();
                }
                catch (JMSException e) {
                }
            }
        }
    }
}
```

And you're ready to let it rip.

## What just happened?

JMS manages queues through templates. Think of a template as a default implementation for the things that you might want to do to a JMS queue, like compose a message. The changes in the context specified your JMS transaction strategy and configured your connection.

You then built the BillingManager class to create a JMS message for each reservation. The application invokes your new method whenever a reservation is created. The JMS template then creates a message. The JMS destinations get handled automatically in the template.

## Testing JMS Applications

Distributed applications are hard to test. It's especially hard to test applications that might have remote behaviors. The good news is that with

Spring, you don't have to actually invoke JMS to retrieve your messages. In this example, you'll learn how to create a stream of messages in the context that can save you the headache of actually creating the JMS infrastructure in every test case.

## How do I do that?

You're going to create a series of messages in the Spring context. Your applications will draw these messages from an array list, instead of actually going across the wire and physically retrieving a JMS message. True, you won't be testing JMS, but you will be able to test the elements of your application that depend on JMS. You'll need to do the following:

- Implement the interface that you use to deal with JMS. In our case, we'll subclass the façade.

- In the new test implementation, draw messages from an array list, rather than from JMS.

- Populate this array list data within the Spring context.

First, let's create a subclass of the façade, for test purposes only (Example 8-16). You'll need to modify the JMS method on the façade. Draw your messages from an array list.

**Example 8-16.** JMSTestRentABike.java

```
private List testBikes;

    public List getTestBikes() {
        return testBikes;
    }

    public void setTestBikes(List testBikes) {
        this.testBikes = testBikes;
    }

    int curBike = 0;

    public Bike getNewBikeFromQueue() {
      try {
        ActiveMQTextMessage m = (ActiveMQTextMessage)testBikes.get(curBike);
        curBike++;
        Bike b = new Bike();
        String s = m.getText();
        String[] vals = s.split(":");
        b.setManufacturer(vals[0]);
        b.setModel(vals[1]);
        return b;
```

**Example 8-16.** JMSTestRentABike.java (continued)

```
    } catch (Exception ex) {
     return null;
    }
}
```

Next, create some sample data in the context (Example 8-17). Instead of distributed messages, your application will get a predictable list of bikes. This context is purely a testing context, so you'll want to store it with your test code rather than with your production contexts.

**Example 8-17.** RentABikeApp-servlet.xml

```xml
<bean id="msg1" class="org.codehaus.activemq.message.ActiveMQTextMessage">
   <property name="text">
      <value>Ventana:El Chamuco</value>
   </property>
</bean>

<bean id="msg2" class="org.codehaus.activemq.message.ActiveMQTextMessage">
   <property name="text">
      <value>Ventana:La Bruja</value>
   </property>
</bean>

<bean id="testBikes" class="java.util.ArrayList">
   <constructor-arg>
      <list>
         <ref local="msg1"/>
         <ref local="msg2"/>
      </list>
   </constructor-arg>
</bean>

<bean id="rentaBikeTarget" class="com.springbook.JMSTestRentABike">
   <property name="storeName"><value>Bruce's Bikes</value></property>
   <property name="sessionFactory"><ref local="sessionFactory"/></property>
   <property name="transactionManager">
      <ref local="transactionManager"/>
   </property>
   <property name="jmsTemplate">
      <ref local="billingJmsTemplate"/>
   </property>
   <property name="testBikes">
      <ref local="testBikes"/>
   </property>
</bean>
```

Finally, create your test case (Example 8-18). Remember to add some logic to terminate the test.

**Example 8-18.** ControllerTest.java

```java
private ApplicationContext ctx;
RentABike store = null;

public void setUp() throws Exception {
    ctx = new FileSystemXmlApplicationContext(
        "/war/WEB-INF/rentaBikeApp-servlet-forJmsTest.xml");
    store = (RentABike)ctx.getBean("rentaBikeTarget");
}

public void testGetBikesFromQueue() throws Exception {
    Bike b = store.getNewBikeFromQueue();
    assertEquals("Ventana", b.getManufacturer());
    assertEquals("El Chamuco", b.getModel());
    b = store.getNewBikeFromQueue();
    assertEquals("Ventana", b.getManufacturer());
    assertEquals("La Bruja", b.getModel());
    b = store.getNewBikeFromQueue();
    assertNull(b);
}
```

After adding this test code, you will likely add more tests that rely on the retrieval of these test messages: for instance, testing the notification consumer to handle the messages retrieved appropriately. The test above just demonstrates that your predetermined messages are being "delivered."

# What just happened?

Messaging systems are notoriously difficult to test. They get markedly easier to handle when you, ahem, inject the ideas of dependency injection and pull test data from a context.

In this specific case, you've got an interface that separates the JMS consumer interface from the implementation. Our testing implementation doesn't go to JMS at all; instead, it pulls data from the context. JMS messages are not the only things that you can test in this way:

- You can build a list of pregenerated random numbers, so your test case is repeatable.

- You can pull a list of times from a list instead of using a timer. This gives you a mechanism to make a timer predictable, again for the purposes of the test.

- You can stub out a database and feed a DAO from a list. This makes it much easier to predictably test the layers that might sit on top of a database. It's also much easier to have separate data sets for contexts that need to test edge conditions.

# Building Rich Clients

I love kayaks. I usually leave canoes to those who prefer them. In that spirit, we leave rich clients to Keith Donald, the founder of the Spring Rich project, for the content and examples in this chapter..

## Getting Started

In this section, you'll start creating a rich client RentABike with an emerging project built directly on the Spring Framework, the Spring Rich Client Project (Spring Rich). The first thing you'll do is get the necessary project files. You'll then see how to get a basic application shell with a splash screen up and running.

But first, a brief background on the aims of the project At its core, Spring Rich is a framework for constructing high-quality, professional Swing-powered desktop applications. It serves several important needs:

*Simplification*

Swing is the most complete Java widget toolkit today, but it's complex and cumbersome. Spring Rich provides a simpler programming model that's easy to leverage and extend.

*Consistency*

Low-level Swing provides no guidelines for constructing consistently well-layered enterprise applications. Through Spring, you get effective J2EE services integration and configuration with a consistent programming model.

*Integration*

Spring Rich integrates the best features of projects like JGoodies, JDNC, JDIC, Webstart, Glazed Lists, Spin, Foxtrot, JIDE, InfoNode, and FlexDock (to name a few), in order to provide a end-to-end platform for rich client development.

# How do I do that?

You first want to get the Spring Rich project. Link to it from the Spring site at *http://www.springframework.org* and follow the directions that you see there. In a nutshell, you will:

1. Access the Spring Rich sourceforge homepage at *http://sourceforge.net/ projects/spring-rich-c*.

2. Access the "Files" tab and select to download the latest "with-dependencies" release archive.

The "with dependencies" release has everything that you need, including Spring Rich and all of its dependencies.

The project is still rapidly evolving, so if you need to download and build the latest CVS snapshot to take advantage of the newest to-be released features, do the following:

1. Connect to the `spring-rich-c` module repository using your favorite CVS plugin. Here are the parameters you'll need:

   Hostname: `cvs.sourceforge.net`
   Repository path: `/cvsroot/spring-rich-c`
   Username: `anonymous`
   Connection type: `pserver`

2. Check out the `spring-richclient` module. If you're using eclipse, you can import this module directly as an eclipse project.

3. Go to the *spring-richclient* root directory and run the *build.xml* file to build *spring-richclient.jar*. Use the *alljars* Ant target.

Now you've got the *spring-richclient.jar*, which you can plug right into your project. You're also going to need a set of image resources. Spring Rich ships a set of out-of-the-box images in *spring-richclient-resources. jar* you can use to jumpstart your UI development. You can also take the images that we packaged with the book's code examples and use them where an example calls for images.

Move the jars into your *lib* directory under your project, and you're off to the races. You'll next configure a splash screen and code a thin application bootstrapper to make sure that things are working.

A startup application context, which hosts services needed at initialization, defines your splash screen (Example 9-1).

**Example 9-1.** startup-context.xml

```
com.springbook.richclient.startup-context.xml

<beans>
```

> Spring Rich ships two distributions for each release: a bare-bones distribution containing the minimal jars, and an all-in-one jar also containing all dependencies.

**Example 9-1.** startup-context.xml (continued)

```xml
<bean id="splashScreen"
        class="org.springframework.richclient.application.SplashScreen">
    <property name="imageResourcePath">
        <value>classpath:/images/splash-screen.jpg</value>
    </property>
</bean>
```

```xml
</beans>
```

Of course, you'll want to get a designer to build you an outrageously cool splash screen, but we all failed art, so you're on your own. In the mean time, you can use a simple JSP like the one in Example 9-2.

**Example 9-2.** splashScreen.jsp

```html
<HTML>
  <BODY>
    Keith's Bikes
  </BODY>
</HTML>
```

You'll then want a simple main driver to kick off loading your application (Example 9-3).

**Example 9-3.** RentABikeLauncher.xml

```java
public class RentABikeLauncher {
    public static void main(String[] args) {
        try {
            String packagePrefix = "com/springbook/richclient";
            String startupContextPath =
                packagePrefix + "/startup-context.xml";
            String[] rootContextPath =
                new String[] {
                    packagePrefix + "/business-layer-definitions.xml",
                    packagePrefix + "/richclient-definitions.xml" };

            new ApplicationLauncher(startupContextPath, rootContextPath);
        }
        catch (Exception e) {
            System.exit(1);
        }
    }
}
```

This thin bootstrapper uses ApplicationLauncher to load your application from the configuration defined in two spring application contexts.

In a standalone rich client environment, you'll typically specify three context configuration files on the classpath. The first configuration file is *startup-context.xml*, which you just defined with your splash screen bean definition. The next two files are *business-layer-definitions.xml* and *rich-client-definitions.xml*. These make up the central root application context, which you will define and configure in the next lab.

You're ready to let it fly.

## What just happened?

Like most rich client apps, Spring Rich-powered apps can take a little bit of time to launch, so the framework lets you put up a splash screen when you launch your application while the user waits. As you've seen, Spring Rich lets you specify the splash-screen configuration in the context.

There's more to it than meets the eye. The framework forks off a thread for you, and loads your application while you look at the pretty splash screen. That way, the user gets the impression of immediate response. This boilerplate code exists in most rich client applications, but is completely managed by the framework.

# Building the Application Shell

Now that you've got Spring Rich up and running, you're ready to configure the main application window. You'll see how to configure the window's command bars, including the menu bar and tool bar. You'll also learn how Spring Rich lets you invoke a centralized GUI command through any number of *actionable controls*, which can trigger some action, like buttons or menu items. You'll also specify a logical command group, which you can reuse in any number of *grouping controls*. These are controls that let you group other actionable controls, like menus or command bars.

Once that soaks in, the following lab shows how to configure the main window's page area. The page will provide the central view into the RentABike inventory.

## High-level application goals

Before going further with implementation, let's clarify the goals of the RentABike rich client that you'll build in this lab.

*The user launches the Bike Store*

The application presents a dazzling splash screen while the application loads.

*The main window displays*

The window's menu bar organizes your user's available commands into logical groups. The window's tool bar provides easy access to frequently needed commands. A "Bike Navigator" component displayed in a central page area provides a view into our current store inventory.

*The user selects an existing bike for editing*

The application presents a form that lets a user update a bike's properties. The form provides validation of the shop's business rules.

*The user adds a new bike*

Doing so displays a wizard, which lets the user enter bike properties validated against our Bike business rules.

Notice a few minor differences between this vision and the web-based clients that you've already used. You've already seen the splash screen. You'll also need to specify the command bars. Later, you'll see the rich validation and forms framework. In this lab, you'll focus on building the main window.

## How do I do that?

To configure your main window, you first need to define several singleton beans that hold the context for your application. As usual, you'll leverage Spring for configuration and dependency injection.

As you've seen, a typical Spring Rich configuration will have three context definitions: a startup context, a root application context, and a child context for each application window. For now, focus on the root application context.

A single root application context defines your logical middle tier (Example 9-4). It's also where several Spring Rich services and descriptors are defined. Typically, the middle-tier business definitions are broken out into their own file, separate from the rich client–tier presentation definitions.

**Example 9-4.** business-layer-definitions.xml

```
<beans>
    <bean name="rentABike" class="com.springbook.ArrayListRentABike">
        <property name="storeName"><value>Keith's Bikes</value></property>
    </bean>
</beans>
```

You've already seen the `RentABike` interface. Notice this context links to the `ArrayListRentABike`, which allows us to build and test the application without any database support (Example 9-5). Later, you'll be able to swap this implementation with one of the database implementations.

**Example 9-5.** com.springbook.richclient.richclient-definitions.xml

```xml
<beans>

    <bean id="application"
     class="org.springframework.richclient.application.Application">
        <constructor-arg index="0">
            <ref bean="applicationDescriptor"/>
        </constructor-arg>
        <constructor-arg index="1">
            <ref bean="applicationLifecycleAdvisor"/>
        </constructor-arg>
    </bean>

    <bean id="applicationDescriptor"
     class="org.springframework.richclient.application.ApplicationDescriptor">
        <property name="name">
            <value>My RentABike</value>
        </property>
        <property name="version">
            <value>1.0</value>
        </property>
    </bean>

    <bean id="applicationLifecycleAdvisor"
     class="com.springbook.richclient.RentABikeLifecycleAdvisor">
        <property name="windowCommandBarDefinitions">
            <value>
                classpath:com/springbook/richclient/window-command-bars.xml
            </value>
        </property>
        <property name="startingPageId">
            <value>bikeNavigator</value>
        </property>
    </bean>
```

> *Spring injects an application descriptor and a lifecycle advisor instance.*

> *The application descriptor provides meta-data, including the application name, and version.*

> *windowCommand-BarDefinitions points to your main window's command bar configuration.*

> *startingPageId is the ID of the page that renders your app's central content pane on startup.*

You see three bean definitions:

Application

The Application class is the central component in a set of application management abstractions in Spring Rich. You'll always define a single application bean for each of your Spring Rich apps.

Application is loaded at startup by the `ApplicationLauncher` to complete the startup initialization process. It issues callbacks at well-defined points within the application's lifecycle to the `ApplicationLifecycleAdvisor` below. It also provides a programmatic API for opening and closing application windows.

ApplicationDescriptor

Each application has an optional *application descriptor,* which provides the application's name, image, caption, description, version, build ID, and other metadata.

ApplicationLifecycleAdvisor

The lifecycle advisor allows convenient customization within well-defined points of a Spring Rich application's lifecycle. For example, before a new window is opened, a callback is issued allowing pre-window display configuration.

The next set of bean definitions select implementations of common services typical of most rich client applications:

*The component factory definition centralizes the production of Swing controls.*

```
<bean id="componentFactory"
 class="org.springframework.richclient.factory.DefaultComponentFactory"/>

<bean id="messageSource"

 class="org.springframework.context.support.ResourceBundleMessageSource">
    <property name="basenames">
      <list>
        <value>org.springframework.richclient.application.messages</value>
        <value>com.springbook.richclient.messages</value>
      </list>
    </property>
</bean>
```

*A Spring message source lets you externalize i18n messages from Java code.*

```
<bean id="imageSource"
 class="org.springframework.richclient.image.DefaultImageSource">
    <property name="basenames">
      <list>
        <value>org.springframework.richclient.application.images</value>
        <value>com.springbook.richclient.images</value>
      </list>
    </property>
    <property name="brokenImageIndicator">
      <value>classpath:/images/alert/error_obj.gif</value>
    </property>
</bean>
```

*An optional Spring Rich Client image source lets you separate hard paths from your code.*

```
<bean id="lookAndFeelConfigurer"
 class="org.springframework.richclient.application.
        config.JGoodiesLooksConfigurer">
    <property name="theme">
      <bean class="com.jgoodies.plaf.plastic.theme.ExperienceBlue"/>
    </property>
</bean>
```

*The optional LooksConfigurer definition lets you control the application's look and feel—in this case, a jgoodies skin.*

The next rich client bean definition deserves special attention because it is a *bean post processor.* Any bean post processor defined in the context will receive a call back after another bean is instantiated by Spring. That callback allows the insertion of custom processing for those beans.

The `applicationObjectConfigurer` post processor below processes all beans that act as factories for controls to be displayed on the screen. Set it up like this, and you'll learn more below:

```
<bean id="applicationObjectConfigurer"
   class="org.springframework.richclient.application.config.
            DefaultApplicationObjectConfigurer">
</bean>
```

This `applicationObjectConfigurer` injects properties to *visual descriptor* beans. Essentially, these beans act as factories for GUI components rendering i18n messages, images, or icons.

To illustrate this in action, consider the `applicationDescriptor` bean you defined above. After Spring instantiates this descriptor, the `applicationObjectConfigurer` injects it localized properties, pulling them from the configured i18n sources.

In summary, the `applicationObjectConfigurer` gives you a powerful, consistent, automated configuration strategy for all of your GUI control factories.

## Check point

Time for a check point. So far in this lab, you've created the root application context defining the business layer and several important rich client services. If you were to run your application now, by launching the `RentABikeApplicationLauncher` main method defined in the first lab, this is what you'd get:

```
org.springframework.richclient.application.ConfigurationException:
  Unable to load window command bar definition at location:
  [classpath: com/springbook/richclient/window-command-bars.xml]
```

The cause is simple. The `RentABikeLifecycleAdvisor` bean points to the above file for the configuration of the main window command bars, but the file doesn't yet exist. It's time to create that file so the main window will load successfully (Example 9-6).

To keep things simple, you'll add a menubar with a single "File" menu for now, and a tool bar with a shared "Save" command.

**Example 9-6.** com.springbook.richclient.window-command-bars.xml

```
<beans>

  <bean id="menuBar"
    class="org.springframework.richclient.command.CommandGroupFactoryBean">
```

*The menu bar will contain the file menu command group.*

```xml
    <property name="members">
      <list>
        <ref bean="fileMenu"/>
      </list>
    </property>
  </bean>

  <bean id="fileMenu"
    class="org.springframework.richclient.command.CommandGroupFactoryBean">
    <property name="members">
      <list>
        <ref bean="newMenu"/>
        <value>separator</value>
        <value>saveCommand</value>
        <value>propertiesCommand</value>
        <value>separator</value>
        <bean class="org.springframework.richclient.command.support.
                    ExitCommand"/>
      </list>
    </property>
  </bean>
```

*The file menu command group has some custom commands and an exit command, which is provided by the framework.*

```xml
  <bean id="sharedTargetableCommandList"
    class="org.springframework.richclient.command.support.CommandList">
    <property name="commandIds">
      <list>
        <value>saveCommand</value>
        <value>propertyCommand</value>
      </list>
    </property>
  </bean>
```

*You'll add a placeholder for the New Bike command, because you haven't implemented it yet.*

```xml
  <bean id="newMenu"
    class="org.springframework.richclient.command.CommandGroupFactoryBean">
    <property name="members">
      <list>
        <value>placeholder:newBikeCommand</value>
      </list>
    </property>
  </bean>
```

*The tool bar will contain the same logical New Menu and Save command as our File menu.*

```xml
  <bean id="toolBar"
    class="org.springframework.richclient.command.CommandGroupFactoryBean">
    <property name="members">
      <list>
        <ref bean="newMenu"/>
        <value>saveCommand</value>
      </list>
    </property>
  </bean>

</beans>
```

That's it! Now if you were to run your application by launching the RentABikeApplicationLauncher main method defined in the first lab, you'd get Figure 9-1.

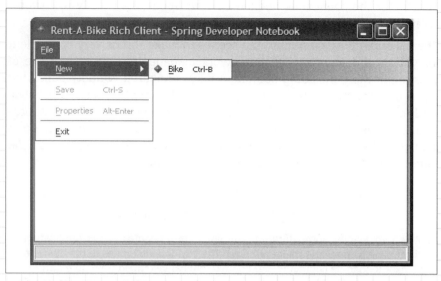

**Figure 9-1.** Rent-A-Bike main method

A generic application shell, with placeholders for our application-specific commands! Pretty easy, huh?!

## What just happened?

How did the framework know that the newBikeCommand should be labeled "Bike" with a "B" mnemonic and a Ctrl-B accelerator key? You certainly didn't define any of that configuration above!

That leads us back to the application object configurer. Just as it can autoconfigure any control factory, it can also autoconfigure commands, pulling i18n metadata from the Spring configured message and image sources. For example, for the newBikeCommand above, the resource bundle files include the following:

```
newBikeCommand.label=&Bike@ctrl B
newBikeCommand.caption=Creates a new bike
newBikeCommand.icon=bullets/blue_diamond.gif
```

The framework handles all the configuration for you. No more manual configuration code!

You saw in this lab how to define the root context of a Spring Rich powered application, and how to configure the main window, including the window's "command bars." The result? A application shell with placeholders for the commands needed by your application, ready to customize in the next lab.

There's a lot going on behind the scenes to make things very convenient for you as a developer. The framework manages the entire lifecycle of your application, including opening a fully configured window populated with the command bars configured in the context file. The slick applicationObjectConfigurer autoconfigures beans for you that produce controls to be displayed on the screen, relieving you from having to configure them manually. In summary, boilerplate code is kept inside the framework, so you can focus on solving your domain problem.

---

## Spring Rich GUI Commands

When your application starts up, the launcher delegates to the Application class, which opens the initial window. The window delegates to the lifecycle advisor to load its command-bar context, typically sourced from an externalized configuration file. Once loaded, the window asks the menuBar command group to produce a fully-populated JMenuBar. The window asks the toolBar command group to produce a fully-populated JToolBar.

Commands are not Swing controls! Commands are *factories* for producing Swing controls bound to a single controller action. ActionCommands produce *actionable* controls like JButtons, JMenuItems, JToggleButtons, JCheckBoxes, and JRadioButtons. CommandGroups produce *grouping* controls, like JMenus, JToolBars, and JMenuBars.

It bears repeating. As with struts, commands are not controls, but are controllers that should execute in response to UI events fired by *bound* controls. Any number of controls can bind to a single action command. Further, any number of grouping controls can bind to a single logical command group. In addition, manipulating the state of a single command automatically updates all bound controls.

This design keeps the Swing controls focused on presentation responsibilities and the signaling of user interface events, while the commands centralize controller logic that executes in response to those events.

---

# Building the Bike Navigator View

Now, you're ready to take the generic application shell you just built and customize the central page area so it displays an interactive "Bike Navigator" component. You'll see how to build the Bike Navigator, which is an implementation of a *view* in Spring Rich terminology. The Spring view is similar to Eclipse RCP's concept of a view.

When you're done, you'll have a interactive view into your bike store's inventory. You'll also have local handlers for the various controller actions (or commands) supported by this view. Specifically, you'll code a local handler for the shared Properties command, which will display the properties of the selected Bike when executed.

## How do I do that?

As you build your BikeNavigator, the first thing you need to do is define a ViewDescriptor for it in configuration code. Each view defined in Spring Rich has a corresponding descriptor. The descriptor, a singleton, provides metadata about the view, including its name, icon, and implementation class. It also acts as a factory for creating view instances of a specific implementation class, as many view instances of the same class can exist on different windows. Note that *views are not singletons*.

```
<bean id="bikeNavigator"
  class="org.springframework.richclient.
      application.support.DefaultViewDescriptor">
    <lookup-method
      name="createView"
      bean="bikeNavigatorViewPrototype"/>
</bean>
```

*You don't see descriptor properties like "name", "image", or "caption" because they are all configured automatically.*

Notice the `<lookup-method>` element. It will override this ViewDescriptor implementation's createView method *at runtime* with a implementation that will return a new bikeNavigatorViewPrototype on each invocation. This lets Spring configure and manage your custom BikeNavigator view instances—which you'll define a specification for next.

Once the ViewDescriptor is defined, you'll create the bean definition and implementation for the BikeNavigator view. This prototype encapsulates

*Views are NOT singletons. Because they're managed by Spring, they can fully leverage dependency injection. You inject the façade here.*

the creation of a graphical view control we select (any Swing JComponent). It also encapsulates the controller logic to coordinate between that control and our RentABike business interface in response to user events. Below is the BikeNavigator bean definition:

```
<bean id="bikeNavigatorViewPrototype"
 class="com.springbook.richclient.BikeNavigator" singleton="false">
    <property name="rentABike">
        <ref bean="rentABike"/>
    </property>
</bean>
</beans>
```

BikeNavigator is a prototype because the same type of view may be active in several application windows at the same time. You cannot share the same view instance because a Swing component can only be a contained within a single Container.

That's it for view configuration code. Now it's time to code the BikeNavigator view implementation and controller logic. You'll inherit from AbstractView, which gives you basic behavior common to all view implementations. For now, you'll only be able to view a list of bikes, and view properties on an existing bike:

*The setter allows configuration of a RentABike reference using standard setter dependency injection.*

*The register-LocalCommand-Executors method attaches local executors to commands.*

*The create-Control method returns the root Swing control realizing this view's UI.*

```
public class BikeNavigator extends AbstractView implements
ApplicationListener {
    private JTree bikesTree;

    private PropertiesCommandExecutor propertiesExecutor =
        new PropertiesCommandExecutor();

    private RentABike rentABike;

    public void setRentABike(RentABike rentABike) {
        this.rentABike = rentABike;
    }

    protected void registerLocalCommandExecutors(
    PageComponentContext context) {
        context.register(GlobalCommandIds.PROPERTIES, propertiesExecutor);
    }

    protected JComponent createControl() {
        initBikesTree();
        return new JScrollPane(bikesTree);
    }

    private void initBikesTree() {
        DefaultMutableTreeNode rootNode = new DefaultMutableTreeNode();

        // get the Bikes from store inventory
        Collection bikes = rentABike.getBikes();
```

```
            // Add tree nodes for each Bike
            for (Iterator it = bikes.iterator(); it.hasNext();) {
                rootNode.add(new DefaultMutableTreeNode(it.next()));
            }

            // Create the Tree Model and JTree implementation
            bikesTreeModel = new DefaultTreeModel(rootNode);
            bikesTree = new JTree(bikesTreeModel);
            bikesTree.setRootVisible(false);
        }

        private class PropertiesCommandExecutor
        extends AbstractActionCommandExecutor {

            private BikeForm bikeForm;

            public PropertiesCommandExecutor() {
                // The command should only be enabled when a single object is
                // selected in the Bike Tree.
                addGuard(new SingleSelectionGuard(bikesTree));
            }

            public void execute() {
                // Create a new Bike Form for editing the selected Bike
                bikeForm = new BikeForm(getSelectedBike());

                // Display the form in a Titled Dialog
                TitledPageApplicationDialog dialog =
                    new TitledPageApplicationDialog(bikeForm, getWindow()) {
                    protected boolean onFinish() {
                        bikeForm.commit();
                        getRentABike().saveBike((Bike)bikeForm.getFormObject());

                        bikesTreeModel.nodeChanged(getSelectedTreeNode());
                        return true;
                    }
                };

                // Display the dialog on the screen
                dialog.showDialog();
            }
        }
    }
}
```

*The Properties-Command-Executor encapsulates controller logic for handling a request to view.*

*The Bike Form will let us edit the selected Bike's properties when the Properties command is executed.*

*Save or update the bike in inventory, using the RentABike façade.*

That's it! You now have a Bike Navigator view defined providing a hierarchical view into current store inventory, realized by a Swing JTree. You also have a *local command executor* for the Properties command defined that will allow the user to edit an existing Bike in inventory using a Bike-Form. In the next lab, you'll implement the BikeForm. You're not quite ready to execute it, because you don't have the full implementation of the property editor yet.

## What just happened?

You just defined the first domain-specific component of the RentABike application, the Bike Navigator View. You saw how views act as control factories for an underlying Swing widget that realizes a navigation function. You also saw how local command executors provide targeted controller logic that is only enabled when certain conditions are satisfied.

It's time to put it all together. Let's walk through the big picture of what "just happens" now when our rich client application starts up:

1. The RentABikeLauncher bootstrapper kicks everything off. It delegates to the ApplicationLauncher framework class, parameterizing the launcher with our startup and root application context definitions.

2. The ApplicationLauncher loads the startup context from the classpath and displays the application splash screen.

3. The ApplicationLauncher creates the root application context from the classpath. It retrieves the "application" singleton from the context to initiate the lifecycle of your RentABike Rich Client.

4. The first major step in the app's lifecycle is to create the main application window displaying the page identified by the startingPageId property. This "starting page" is the bikeNavigator. For your application, you only have a single page with a single view defined.

5. Once the framework creates the window, the Application-LifecycleAdvisor loads the windowCommandBarDefinitions configuration. The window creates and populates its menu bar, tool bar, page area, and status bar.

6. The window is opened and displayed. The window's command bars and the central page area containing your new Bike Navigator View are displayed (Figure 9-2).

The properties command is bound to the execute() method that we added to the PropertiesCommandExecutor inner class in the Bike-Navigator controller. When you select a bike and hit the ALT-ENTER key, Spring Rich looks for the command executor that's bound to targetable Properties command and executes it.

# Building the Bike Editor Forms

So far, the application looks good, but it doesn't do too much that's useful. You still need to create a BikeForm to display in a titled dialog, allowing

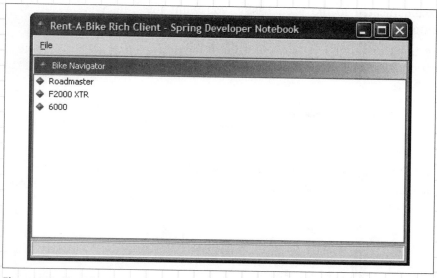

**Figure 9-2.** The Bike Store application main page has amenities, such as a menu bar

the editing of properties on an existing bike. The same form will need to be used to add a new bike to store inventory.

In general the forms framework, with the data binding and validation framework, are three of the fundamental strengths of the Spring Rich Client Project.

## How do I do that?

To create your bike form, you'll first define the declarative validation rules for the Bike class. These rules will be defined *independent* of any presentation code, so they can easily be reused in different environments.

After that, you'll see how to implement the BikeForm itself, and how the framework auto-binds form controls to backing domain object properties for you, with as-you-type validation.

Finally, you'll review the BikeForm integration with the Properties-CommandExecutor defined in the previous lab (for editing an existing Bike), and see how to reuse the BikeForm in a NewBikeWizard in order to add new bikes to store inventory.

### Validation

When a user edits or adds a bike, you want the framework to validate any new data. Furthermore, you want any validation errors to be clearly communicated to the user. Lastly, you want the framework to prevent forms that contain validation errors from being submitted.

To hook in validation rules, add the following bean to your root application context:

```
<beans>

    <bean id="rulesSource"
          class="com.springbook.richclient.RentABikeValidationRulesSource"/>

</beans>
```

The above definition selects an implementation of the RulesSource interface that defines validation rules for the domain entities of your RentABike application. The implementation is surprisingly simple:

```
com.springbook.richclient.RentABikeValidationRulesSource

public class RentABikeValidationRulesSource extends DefaultRulesSource {
    public ValidationRulesSource() {
        addRules(createBikeRules());
    }

    private Rules createBikeRules() {
        return new Rules(Bike.class) {
            protected void initRules() {
                addRequired("model", maxLength(25));
                add("weight", gt(0.0));
                add("frame", range(0, 100));
                addRequired("serialNo", regexp("[0-9a-fA-f]*"));
            }
        };
    }
}
```

The createBikeRules() factory method creates the validation rules for your Bike domain object. The initRules() callback adds the following constraints on a Bike's properties:

- The model property is required and has a max length of 25.
- The weight property must be greater than 0.0.
- The frame property must be in the range 0 to 100, inclusive.
- The serialNo property is required and must match the provided regular expression.

You now need to implement the form that will be used to add and edit bikes, of course. This form will enforce the above validation rules, and will only be enabled for submit when there are no validation errors:

**Chapter 9: Building Rich Clients**

```java
public class BikeForm extends AbstractForm {

    public BikeForm(Bike bike) {
        super(bike);
    }

    public BikeForm(FormModel bikeFormModel) {
        super(bikeFormModel);
    }

    protected JComponent createFormControl() {
        TableFormBuilder formBuilder = new TableFormBuilder(getFormModel());
        formBuilder.add("manufacturer");
        formBuilder.row();
        formBuilder.add("model");
        formBuilder.row();
        formBuilder.add("frame");
        formBuilder.row();
        formBuilder.add("serialNo");
        formBuilder.row();
        formBuilder.add("weight");
        formBuilder.row();
        formBuilder.add("status",
            getFormModel().createBoundComboBox("status", Bike.STATUSES));
        return formBuilder.getForm();
    }

}
```

Pretty simple, huh? I can't imagine building form creation being much simpler than this! The `TableFormBuilder` above automatically selects, creates, and binds editing controls for each of the Bike's domain object properties. These include the manufacturer, model, frame, serial number, weight, and status. The builder also produces properly aligned labels with mnemonics for each form field. Finally, the form provides as-you-type-validation for each field, enforcing the declarative validation rules you just configured!

Now let's revisit your `PropertiesCommandExecutor` implementation to see again how the `BikeForm` displays the properties of a selected Bike in the `BikeNavigator` view:

```java
private class PropertiesCommandExecutor
extends AbstractActionCommandExecutor {

    private BikeForm bikeForm;

    public PropertiesCommandExecutor() {
        // The command should only be enabled when a single object is
        // selected in the Bike Tree.
        addGuard(new SingleSelectionGuard(bikesTree));
    }
```

*The Bike Form will let us edit the selected Bike's properties when the Properties command is executed.*

```
public void execute() {
    // Create a new Bike Form for editing the selected Bike
    bikeForm = new BikeForm(getSelectedBike());

    // Display the form in a Titled Dialog
    TitledPageApplicationDialog dialog =
        new TitledPageApplicationDialog(bikeForm, getWindow()) {
        protected boolean onFinish() {
            bikeForm.commit();
            getRentABike().saveBike((Bike)bikeForm.getFormObject());
            bikesTreeModel.nodeChanged(getSelectedTreeNode());
            return true;
        }
    };

    // Display the dialog on the screen
    dialog.showDialog();
    }
    }
}
```

*Save or update the bike in inventory, using the RentABike façade. Notify the Bike Tree that the selected node may have changed.*

You now have the form fully integrated with the Properties-CommandExecutor of the BikeNavigator view. When Properties is invoked on a selected Bike in the navigator tree, the BikeForm will be displayed, as in Figure 9-3.

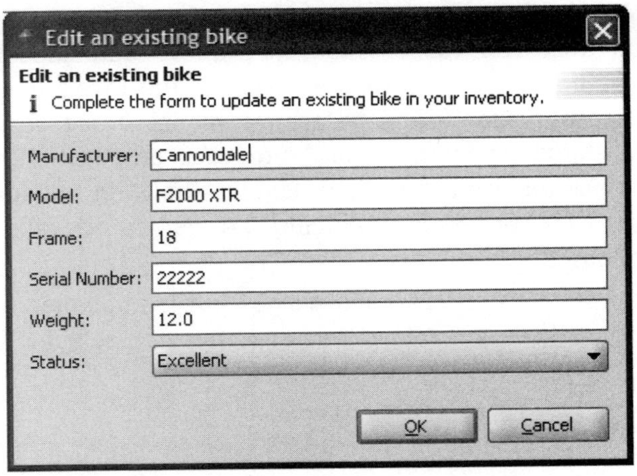

**Figure 9-3.** BikeForm

Now you'll want this same Form to be *reused* for creating new Bikes. You'll want to go back to Lab 2, where you created a New Menu command group displayed in the File menu and on the Toolbar. This New Menu group contained a single action command placeholder for the New

Bike command. You're now ready to replace that placeholder with a real command instance, which will be a `TargetableActionCommand` pointing to a "New Bike Wizard."

Recall:

```
com.springbook.richclient.window-command-bars.xml

<bean id="newMenu"
 class="org.springframework.richclient.command.CommandGroupFactoryBean">
  <property name="members">
    <list>
        <value>placeholder:newBikeCommand</value>
    </list>
  </property>
</bean>
```

*You'll add a placeholder for the New Bike command, because you haven't implemented it yet.*

You'll replace the placeholder with:

```
com.springbook.richclient.window-command-bars.xml

<bean id="newMenu"
 class="org.springframework.richclient.command.CommandGroupFactoryBean">
  <property name="members">
    <list>
        <ref bean="newBikeCommand"/>
    </list>
  </property>
</bean>
```

*Point to the "real" New Bike command.*

```
<bean id="newBikeCommand"
 class="org.springframework.richclient.command.TargetableActionCommand">
  <property name="commandExecutor"/>
      <ref bean="newBikeWizard"/>
  </property>
</bean>
```

*Target the command at the New Bike Wizard. The wizard acts the Action-CommandExecutor for this command.*

And of course, you can't forget the definition of the actual `NewBikeWizard` itself. Note the wizard should be defined in `richclient-definitions.xml` because it is a singleton service shared by all windows:

```
com.springbook.richclient.richclient-definitions.xml

<bean id="newBikeWizard"
 class="com.springbook.richclient.NewBikeWizard">
    <property name="rentABike">
      <ref bean="rentABike"/>
    </property>
</bean>
```

The `NewBikeWizard` provides the workflow required to add a new Bike to inventory. On finish (submit), this wizard uses the `rentABike` to save the new Bike to the database.

*The wizard dialog that realizes the Wizard UI.*

So what does the wizard work? Take a look at the code for the NewBikeWizard in Example 9-7. By now, the consistency and simplicity of the programming model should really stand out.

**Example 9-7.** The wizard took less than 25 lines of code, plus an additional few lines for validation

```
public class NewBikeWizard extends AbstractWizard implements
ActionCommandExecutor {
    private WizardDialog wizardDialog;
    private FormModel formModel;
    private RentABike rentABike;
    public NewBikeWizard() {
        super("newBikeWizard");
    }
    public void setRentABike(RentABike rentABike) {
        this.rentABike = rentABike;
    }
    public void addPages() {
        addForm(new BikeForm(formModel));
    }
    public void execute() {
        if (wizardDialog == null) {
            wizardDialog = new WizardDialog(this);
            formModel = SwingFormModel.createFormModel(new Bike());
        } else {
            // reset the form to a new, "fresh" Bike instance
            formModel.reset();
        }
        wizardDialog.showDialog();
    }

    protected boolean onFinish() {
        Bike newBike = (Bike)getNewBike();
        getRentABike().saveBike(newBike);
        return true;
    }

    private Bike getNewBike() {
        formModel.commit();
        return (Bike)formModel.getFormObject();
    }
}
```

*The form model for the wizard uses a compound form to edit a single domain object across multiple pages.*

*The RentABike business facade.*

*This code adds all of the wizard's pages.*

*Execute this wizard, display-ing a wizard dialog for editing a new Bike.*

*Perform the wizard "finish" action, saving the new Bike to the database using the RentABike business façade.*

## What just happened?

You just built a BikeForm for editing the properties of existing Bikes, as well as new Bikes that have yet to be added to store inventory. You learned how to define validation rules enforced by the Form during the editing process, and how to launch the Form for display in command (controller) execution logic. Finally, you gained a brief insight into Spring Rich's wizard framework.

Now if you access the File → New → Bike command from the Menu Bar, you'll see Figure 9-4. Select the Bike menu item, and the newBikeCommand invokes the execute( ) method on the NewBikeWizard, an ActionCommandExecutor. A WizardDialog then pops up displaying a BikeForm for editing a new Bike domain object, as in Figure 9-5. If the user selects Finish, edits are committed to the backing form object and the new Bike is saved to the database. If the user chooses to Cancel, nothing happens.

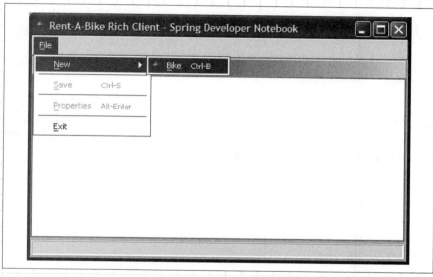

**Figure 9-4.** New bike

When a property has a validation error, the Finish button is disabled and an visual indicator is shown along with a descriptive error message. Once all validation constraints are satisfied, the validation error is removed and Finish becomes enabled.

## What about...

...other Spring frameworks? In this book, we've tried to give you a taste of the most exciting open source project to come along since Hibernate. It's not a complete picture, though. Spring also integrates workflow, management through JMX, dynamic languages with Groovy, richer AOP through AspectJ, and many other frameworks. More projects come monthly.

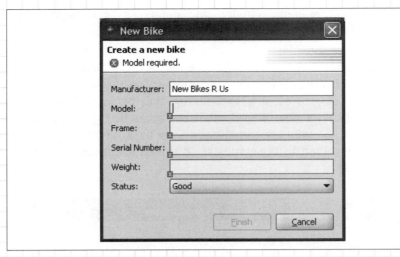

**Figure 9-5.** Create new bike

But you do have all of the tools at your disposal to know how to integrate them. You've seen how to structure a typical web application. You've learned to attach services to your business logic, adopt a new GUI framework, switch persistence strategies, and write a test with a mock, stub, or POJO. Now, we urge you to stay with Spring through one full development cycle. By doing development, testing, deployment and maintenance with Spring, you'll see just how much of a difference that it can make for you.

# Index

We'd like to hear your suggestions for improving our indexes. Send email to *index@oreilly.com*.

## G

grouping controls, Spring Rich, 167
GUI commands, Spring Rich, 174

## H

Hessian, 153
Hibernate, 5, 81, 96
    alternatives, 102
    flow, 101
    management, 102
    mapping, 102
    persistence and, 96
    properties, 98
    standards, 102
    templates, 99
    testing and, 102
HTTP
    Burlap, 153
    Hessian, 153
HTTP invokers, 153

## I

iBATIS, 81
    facade, 83
    installation, 82
    integration, 82
    OR mapping, 89
    Oracle and, 88
    templates, 89
    transactions, 89
identifiers, tables, 63
installation
    EasyMock, 77
    iBATIS, 82
    Kodo, 91
    MySQL, 62
instance-based security, 146
integration, Spring Rich, 164
interceptor strategy, 106
    objects, 110
interceptors
    ACEGI and, 146
    as objects, 121
    testing and, 147
    (see also advice)
interfaces
    advice building, 106
    dependency injection and, 6

MailSender, 151
ThrowsAdvice, 117
italic text in book, xi
iteration, JDBC result set, 69

## J

Java, 5
JavaMailSender implementation, 151
JDBC
    callback classes, 68
    configuration, 66
    control inversion, 66
    drivers, MySQL and, 62
    exceptions
        folding, 69
        low-level management, 69
        unchecked, 66
    iteration, result set, 69
    query parameters, 68
    resource management, 66, 69
    templates, 65
        queries, 68
    transactions, 69
JdbcDaoSupport class, 66
JdbcTemplate, error handling and, 68
JDO, 81
    Kodo, 90
    persistent model creation, 91
    PersistentManager, 91
    PersistentManagerFactory, 91
JMS
    application testing, 160
    remoting, 156
    templates, 160
JSF (JavaServer Faces), 51
    expression language, 51
    navigation rules, 57
    Spring integration, 58
    value bindings, 51
    views, 53
JSP layer, Web MVC, 22
JUnit, 5
JUnit tests, validation, 49
JUnitTest, subclasses, 15

## K

Kodo, 90
    download, 91
    installation, 91
    Launch the Workbench wizard, 92

## About the Authors

**Bruce A. Tate** is a kayaker, mountain biker, and father of two. In his spare time, he is an independent consultant in Austin, Texas. In 2001, he founded J2Life, LLC, a consulting firm that specializes in Java persistence frameworks and lightweight development methods. His customers have included FedEx, Great West Life, TheServerSide, and BEA. He speaks at conferences and Java user's groups around the nation. Before striking out on his own, Bruce spent 13 years at IBM working on database technologies, object-oriented infrastructure, and Java. He was recruited away from IBM to help start the client services practice in an Austin startup called Pervado Systems. He later served a brief stint as CTO of IronGrid, which built nimble Java performance tools. Bruce is the author of four books, including the best-selling *Bitter Java* (Manning) and the Jolt-winning *Better, Faster, Lighter Java* (O'Reilly). First rule of kayak: when in doubt, paddle like hell.

Working as a professional programmer, instructor, speaker, and pundit since 1992, **Justin Gehtland** has developed real-world applications using VB, COM, .NET, Java, Perl, and a slew of obscure technologies since relegated to the trash heap of technical history. His focus has historically been on "connected" applications, which of course has led him down the COM+, ASP/ASP.NET, and JSP roads.

Justin is the co-author of *Effective Visual Basic* (Addison Wesley) and *Windows Forms Programming in Visual Basic .NET* (Addison Wesley). He is currently the regular "Agility" columnist on *The Server Side .NET*, and works as a consultant through his company Relevance, LLC, in addition to teaching for DevelopMentor.

## Colophon

Our look is the result of reader comments, our own experimentation, and feedback from distribution channels. Distinctive covers complement our distinctive approach to technical topics, breathing personality and life into potentially dry subjects.

The *Developer's Notebook* series is modeled on the tradition of laboratory notebooks. Laboratory notebooks are an invaluable tool for researchers and their successors.

The purpose of a laboratory notebook is to facilitate the recording of data and conclusions as the work is being conducted, creating a faithful and immediate history. The notebook begins with a title page that includes the owner's name and the subject of research. The pages of the notebook should be numbered and prefaced with a table of contents. Entries must be clear, easy to read, and accurately dated; they should use simple, direct language to indicate the name of the experiment and the steps taken. Calculations are written out carefully and relevant thoughts and ideas recorded. Each experiment is introduced and summarized as it is added to the notebook. The goal is to produce comprehensive, clearly organized notes that can be used as a reference. Careful documentation creates a valuable record and provides a practical guide for future developers.

Colleen Gorman was the production editor and proofreader for *Spring: A Developer's Notebook*. Genevieve d'Entremont and Claire Cloutier provided quality control. Johnna VanHoose Dinse wrote the index.

Emma Colby designed the cover of this book, based on a series design by Edie Freedman. Karen Montgomery produced the cover layout with Adobe InDesign CS using the Officina Sans and JuniorHandwriting fonts.

David Futato and Edie Freedman designed the interior layout. This book was converted by Judy Hoer to FrameMaker 5.5.6 with a format conversion tool created by Erik Ray, Jason McIntosh, Neil Walls, and Mike Sierra that uses Perl and XML technologies. The text font is Adobe Boton; the heading font is ITC Officina Sans; the code font is LucasFont's TheSans Mono Condensed, and the handwriting font is a modified version of JuniorHandwriting made by Tepid Monkey Foundry, and modified by O'Reilly. The illustrations that appear in the book were produced by Robert Romano, Jessamyn Read, and Lesley Borash using Macromedia FreeHand MX and Adobe Photoshop CS. This colophon was written by Colleen Gorman.

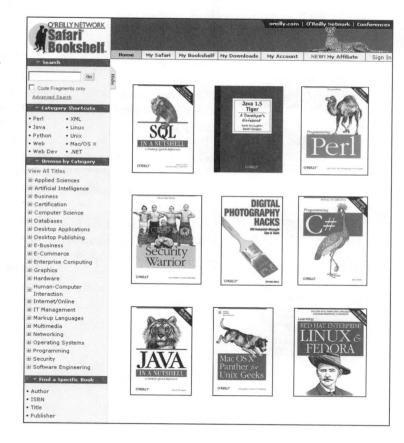

# Related Titles Available from O'Reilly

## Java

Ant: The Definitive Guide

Better, Faster, Lighter Java

Eclipse

Eclipse Cookbook

Enterprise JavaBeans,
4th Edition

Hardcore Java

Head First Java

Head First Servlets & JSP

Head First EJB

Hibernate:
A Developer's Notebook

J2EE Design Patterns

Java 1.5 Tiger:
A Developer's Notebook

Java & XML Data Binding

Java & XML

Java Cookbook, *2nd Edition*

Java Data Objects

Java Database Best Practices

Java Enterprise Best Practices

Java Enterprise in a Nutshell,
*2nd Edition*

Java Examples in a Nutshell,
*3rd Edition*

Java Extreme Programming
Cookbook

Java in a Nutshell, *4th Edition*

Java Management Extensions

Java Message Service

Java Network Programming,
*2nd Edition*

Java NIO

Java Performance Tuning,
*2nd Edition*

Java RMI

Java Security, *2nd Edition*

JavaServer Faces

Java ServerPages, *2nd Edition*

Java Servlet & JSP Cookbook

Java Servlet Programming,
*2nd Edition*

Java Swing, *2nd Edition*

Java Web Services in a Nutshell

Learning Java, *2nd Edition*

Mac OS X for Java Geeks

Programming Jakarta Struts
*2nd Edition*

Tomcat: The Definitive Guide

WebLogic:
The Definitive Guide

# Keep in touch with O'Reilly

## 1. Download examples from our books

To find example files for a book, go to:

*www.oreilly.com/catalog*

select the book, and follow the "Examples" link.

## 2. Register your O'Reilly books

Register your book at *register.oreilly.com*

Why register your books?
Once you've registered your O'Reilly books you can:

- Win O'Reilly books, T-shirts or discount coupons in our monthly drawing.
- Get special offers available only to registered O'Reilly customers.
- Get catalogs announcing new books (US and UK only).
- Get email notification of new editions of the O'Reilly books you own.

## 3. Join our email lists

Sign up to get topic-specific email announcements of new books and conferences, special offers, and O'Reilly Network technology newsletters at:

*elists.oreilly.com*

It's easy to customize your free elists subscription so you'll get exactly the O'Reilly news you want.

## 4. Get the latest news, tips, and tools

*www.oreilly.com*

- "Top 100 Sites on the Web"—PC Magazine
- CIO Magazine's Web Business 50 Awards

Our web site contains a library of comprehensive product information (including book excerpts and tables of contents), downloadable software, background articles, interviews with technology leaders, links to relevant sites, book cover art, and more.

## 5. Work for O'Reilly

Check out our web site for current employment opportunities:

*jobs.oreilly.com*

## 6. Contact us

O'Reilly Media
1005 Gravenstein Hwy North
Sebastopol, CA 95472 USA
TEL:   707-827-7000 or 800-998-9938
          (6am to 5pm PST)
FAX:   707-829-0104

**order@oreilly.com**
For answers to problems regarding your order or our products. To place a book order online, visit:

*www.oreilly.com/order_new*

**catalog@oreilly.com**
To request a copy of our latest catalog.

**booktech@oreilly.com**
For book content technical questions or corrections.

**corporate@oreilly.com**
For educational, library, government, and corporate sales.

**proposals@oreilly.com**
To submit new book proposals to our editors and product managers.

**international@oreilly.com**
For information about our international distributors or translation queries. For a list of our distributors outside of North America check out:

*international.oreilly.com/distributors.html*

**adoption@oreilly.com**
For information about academic use of O'Reilly books, visit:

*academic.oreilly.com*